CAN THESE BONES LIVE?

More Praise for *Can These Bones Live?*

"In a culture inundated with simplistic, prescriptive, quick-fix books for church leadership and congregational revitalization, it is refreshing to encounter an honest voice that reminds us that a healthy church requires more than warm bodies in our pews and a wide variety of church activities. Kevass Harding shares a story of hard work, prayerful discernment, and a commitment to change that deals with the real costs of faithful discipleship."
—Dan R. Dick, Research Coordinator, General Board of Discipleship of The United Methodist Church

"This is a must read for pastors, laity, and any church leaders who want to experience revitalization! With the leadership principles he learned, Kevass answers a resounding YES—dry bones can live again!
—Tyrone D. Gordon, Senior Pastor, St. Luke "Community" United Methodist Church in Dallas, Texas

"Kevass Harding has made a thoughtful contribution to the search for renewal of spiritual life in the face of the decline of 'mainline' churches. His study is solid, innovative, convincing, and eminently practical."
—Laurence L. Welborn, Professor of New Testament, United Theological Seminary

KEVASS J. HARDING

CAN THESE BONES LIVE?

BRINGING NEW LIFE TO A DYING CHURCH

Abingdon Press
Nashville

CAN THESE BONES LIVE?
BRINGING NEW LIFE TO A DYING CHURCH

Copyright © 2007 by Abingdon Press

This book is printed on acid-free paper.

Library of Congress Cataloging-in-Publication Data

Harding, Kevass J., 1967–
  Can these bones live? : bringing new life to a dying church / Kevass J. Harding.
    p. cm.
  ISBN-13: 978-0-687-33557-2 (pbk. : alk. paper)
  1. Church renewal. 2. Church growth. I. Title.

  BV600.3.H44 2007
  287′.678186—dc22

                                                                2006023485

All scripture quotations unless noted otherwise are taken from the *New Revised Standard Version of the Bible*, copyright 1989 by the Division of Christian Education of the National Council of the Churches of Christ in the United States of America. Used by permission. All rights reserved.

Scripture quotations marked (KJV) are from the King James or Authorized Version of the Bible.

07 08 09 10 11 12 13 14 15 16—10 9 8 7 6 5 4 3 2 1

MANUFACTURED IN THE UNITED STATES OF AMERICA

To my beautiful and wonderful wife, Teketa, whom since August 27, 1994, I think of on two occasions—day and night. I truly thank you for all of your words of encouragement, support, and prayers during the writing of this book. You are truly a godsend. I love you.

To my son, Carnez, and my daughter, Makayla, you are my outstanding and gifted children. I am so proud to be your father. You're both a blessing from God. Thank you for your patience and understanding during the writing of this book.

To my mom, Sharron, who has loved me unconditionally from the moment I was born. I thank you for all your words of advice and wisdom.

To my deceased father, Ervin, I wish we could have had more time together; however, I will always cherish our short time together; love, your son.

To my sister, Shawnteé, my brother-in-law, Joseph, and my nieces Tiara and Teala, I thank you for always making Dallas a home away from home when we visit. I love you all.

To my brother Richard, who shared a bedroom with me for eighteen years. I will always cherish our childhood. Thank you for my beautiful niece Jada; she is music from heaven.

To my "Big Brother" Cliff, who has been more like a father than a brother, I love you and respect you from the bottom of my heart. Thank you for all that you have done and continue to do for me.

To my mother-in-law, Anniece, who has been a tremendous supporter of me and my ministry. I thank you for giving birth to my beautiful wife.

To Denise, my sister-in-law; my nieces Teketa Jr. and Daisha; I love and thank all three of you for your wonderful support.

To my brother and sister-in-law Dennis and Claudia, along with their three children, Sheena, Kapten, and Kaitlyn; thank you for your love and support.

To my two adopted nieces Triniece and Aiyana, I love you both. You are both dear and special to my heart.

To my grandmother, all my uncles, aunts, cousins, and relatives; I love you and may God bless you all.

To my deceased maternal grandfather, my deceased paternal grandmother and aunt, I will always love you and cherish your memories.

To my extended family called Dellrose United Methodist Church; without you this book would have been impossible. It has been through our relationship of building community that I have discovered God can take little and do much in the life of any church, regardless of size. God bless you all.

CONTENTS

FOREWORD

Change is hard. We know that is true in our personal lives, our work lives, and our families.

In some ways, change is most difficult for religious communities that seek to connect with God and to give expression to the deepest values of our faith. For congregations that have carried out significant ministry in a particular neighborhood for many decades, there is a community memory that hopes and believes the future will be like the past and the wonderful days of former times can be carried forward with only incremental change. In such cases we want to carry out our ministry with only minimal adaptations. We prefer development that builds incrementally on the past.

For many congregations, however, that developmental trajectory is not possible. For some, populations are declining. For others, younger people have different cultural values and experience the presence of God in new and different media. For many, competition from television, entertainment, and the Internet poses challenges. For others, demographic changes lead to the presence of new racial and ethnic groups moving into the area. When you list the types of congregations facing demographic changes, one would include those in inner cities, rural areas, county-seat towns, and suburbs.

As bishop of the Kansas Area of The United Methodist Church, I have repeatedly said that too many of our congregations are fully prepared to grow if the 1950s ever come back. We all know that they are not coming back, and that ministry in the twenty-first century will be quite different from those practices that were successful fifty years ago. Many congregations face the stark choice of changing or dying.

Why would a church go through the heartrending and mentally challenging path of radical change? Kevass Harding and Dellrose United Methodist Church did it for Jesus. They did it out of faithfulness to the gospel and God's call to make disciples of Jesus Christ.

This book chronicles the journey that Pastor Harding and the congregation traveled from near death to exuberant vitality. It is frank about the difficulties, including "the great exodus" of persons who could not make the necessary transition. It is clear about the contextual nature of worship and evangelism and how the church had to be relevant to its new target population. The book's biblical basis for ministry is apparent in every chapter. It is clear about not shooting for success, but seeking to disciple believers. The growth and vitality of Dellrose today are the by-product of a Spirit-filled and mission-minded approach to ministry that can inspire many of us to similar paths in our places of service.

Throughout the book, Harding is careful to give God the credit for taking what was only a little and making much of it. He is also focused on reaching, teaching, and sending a formula that cogently summarizes the process of making disciples of Jesus Christ.

I have been blessed every time I have worshiped with the Dellrose congregation, and I hope the insights in this book will be a blessing to others seeking to adapt faithfully to a changing world.

Scott J. Jones
Bishop, Kansas Area
August 21, 2006

INTRODUCTION

WHEN LITTLE IS MUCH

T here is a boy here who has five barley loaves and two fish. But what are they among so many people?" (John 6:9). Feeding five thousand people with two fish and five loaves of bread is truly a story about "Signs of Hope." A hope of how Jesus took little and made much. And even today, Jesus is still taking little and making much.

Regardless of what statistics might indicate about The United Methodist Church being a dying church, with a graying membership and declining roll, I see other signs. One sign of hope is at Dellrose United Methodist Church, located in Wichita, Kansas. Yes, at Dellrose, I see a Spirit of God moving with zeal and aspiration that cannot be touched by statistics alone.

At Dellrose I see signs of active ministry, not maintenance. At Dellrose I see signs of a thriving church, not a slowly dying church in the grasp of institutional death. At Dellrose I see signs in new Sunday school classes, new Bible study groups, new worship styles, and more and more people boldly living faithfully for Jesus Christ. At Dellrose I see signs of organized small-group fellowships, outreach ministries for the entire community, a youth center called "De La Rosa," and a counseling center to help those who struggle with the vices of the world. At Dellrose I see a vital congregation no longer playing church, but, through its vision and mission, being church—focused more on relationships than on structure and organization.

These signs did not appear overnight. There was no magic potion or six-steps-to-success book. Resources were limited, encouraging words were few, doubt was bountiful, anger stood nearby, and fear ran rampant. Yet Jesus, just as in the feeding of the five thousand, took little and made much at Dellrose.

In the fall of 1997, I was an associate pastor at Saint Mark United Methodist Church in Wichita, Kansas, and a seminary student at Phillips Theological Seminary in Enid, Oklahoma. Upon arriving home one night, my wife, Teketa, informed me the district superintendent had just called and wanted me to return his call when I got home. Although I was weary and exhausted from the commute—an hour-and-a-half drive, one way—I quickly returned his call.

He informed me he had a new appointment for me at Dellrose United Methodist Church, one mile east of Saint Mark United Methodist Church. Dellrose was a declining church with a predominantly white, graying membership, sitting right in the middle of a rapidly growing, working-middle-class, predominantly black neighborhood.

In the late 1980s, a transition had begun to take place in the church and in the neighborhood. The church members began to age, and the community began to transition from white to black. During this transition, membership and attendance fell drastically. In the early to mid-1970s, worship attendance was approximately 300–500. By 1992, attendance was 124. This was truly a church in the throes of institutional death.

During this time, some of the members of the Dellrose Church put together a study group to see how the church could overcome the obstacles before them. The group concluded that if they wanted to continue to do ministry, they would have to alter their ministry and worship styles to meet the needs of the new community. The first attempt, made in the early 1990s, was not successful. The second attempt was made in 1998 when I was appointed as pastor to Dellrose United Methodist Church. When I arrived on August 5, 1998, membership was 131, with an average worship attendance of 63.

During my introductory meeting with the staff-parish relations committee and the district superintendent, I was advised it was time for the church to make the transition to effectively minister to the surrounding neighborhood and community. I understood this to mean that the church was prepared to follow the guidance for transitional change from the 1996 *United Methodist Book of Discipline*:

> When the communities where the church is located experience transition especially identified as economic and or ethnic, the local church shall engage in deliberate analysis of the neighborhood change and alter its programs to meet the needs and cultural patterns of the new residents. The local church shall make every effort to remain in the neighborhood and develop effective ministries to those who are newcomers, whether of a cultural, economic, or ethnic group different from the original or present members.[1]

However, I soon discovered that when some people talk about transition, that is all it is—talk! As soon as we began to alter Dellrose's programs to meet the needs and cultural patterns of the new residents, we were met with strong opposition from many of the original members. The opposition was so strong that it sometimes brought tears to my eyes. The people complained just as the children of Israel at the Red Sea complained to Moses, "What have you done to us, bringing us out of Egypt?" (Exodus 14:11b). They complained that the transition was too fast. If we didn't stop, they would leave, believing that their action would hurt the church financially.

September 1998 marked the beginning of the exodus of these members. Except for three households, all of the members withdrew, transferred, or removed their membership, leaving Dellrose to fail. By December of 1998, the total membership was 25. God, however, did not leave Dellrose to fail!

Signs of Hope

Throughout the time of trial and transition, I saw signs of hope and new life. Those signs included the support of my wife and family, new members of Dellrose, some of my colleagues, and my district superintendent. They will always have my gratitude and love.

Worship

One of the **first signs** of hope came when Dellrose changed its worship style to reach the lost. Our music now is lively, heavy on rhythm. We use many leaders in worship to keep it fresh. I preach sermons that are focused on faith, and relevant to the issues that are significant to the young, transient and stable, multiethnic, working, blue-collar community. We ask special groups and soloists from the community to sing, varying the groups and music weekly. The length of worship is immaterial, although services tend to last an hour and a half. Average weekly worship attendance has grown from 63 to 400.

Teaching

Once people started coming and joining Dellrose through our worship experience, the **second sign** of hope was teaching the found through church school. We started this with the program "Sunday School: It's for Life." Starting with our small Sunday school, we now have seven DISCIPLE Bible study groups, midweek Bible study, and small-group ministries for men, women, children, singles, and couples.

Ministry

The **third sign** of hope was sending the taught, living our faith and reaching others through ministries and outreach. Dellrose's youth and counseling centers have healed and allowed many people to have a personal relationship with Jesus Christ. Personally, I believe that through our outreach ministries, we have reached people we never would have reached any other way. These ministries have allowed signs of hope to shine throughout the church and community.

These are just some of the signs of hope at Dellrose. I can safely say that since my first Sunday in January 1999, and since Dellrose has transitioned to meet the needs of the community, someone has joined the church every Sunday. The active membership has grown from 25 to more than 600 members, and the average attendance has grown from 63 to 400. The annual budget has grown from $1,500 a Sunday to more than $5,000 a Sunday. No longer is the Sunday morning experience considered a "church service"; rather, the Sunday morning experience is a "worship celebration," where the people of God come together celebrating the goodness of God and then leave together to serve just as Christ has commissioned us to do.

In Ezekiel 37, the prophet goes into a valley of dry bones. The bones represent past lives from a different time. God asks Ezekiel, "Mortal, can these bones live?" (Ezekiel 37:3). Can there be life again, where there is now death? Are revitalization and transformation possible? Can Dellrose be transitioned and revived into a vital congregation where a relationship with Jesus Christ is more important than having your name on the membership roll? To all those questions, God says yes!

Yes, in the hands of God, with much faith, vision, prayer, commitment, and hard work, little can become much. However, little did not become much overnight. There were some sleepless nights; sometimes I cried in the middle of the night, tossing and turning, praying God would take this cup, called Dellrose United Methodist Church, away from me. But Jesus took little and began to make much at Dellrose in the areas of worship, discipleship, and ministry/leadership. We will look more deeply at each of these areas in turn throughout the book.

God says yes, we can live. From out of the ashes, I see and believe there are signs of hope at Dellrose and in The United Methodist Church. What we must do as a church is allow Jesus Christ to be our first love and let him do the same thing he did with the two fish and five loaves of bread. When we have faith and do this, Jesus can take little and make much, truly, a sign of hope. Amen!

CHAPTER ONE

THE MAIN THING

*The hand of the LORD came upon me, and he brought me
out by the spirit of the LORD and set me down in the middle of a valley; it was full of bones . . . He said to me,
"Mortal, can these bones live?" (Ezekiel 37:1, 3)*

Jesus is still in the business of breathing new life into our
churches today. I write this book to remind the people of
God, clergy and laity, of that. Regardless of the size of your
church; regardless of what statistics indicate about how The
United Methodist Church is dying, with a graying membership
and declining roll; regardless if church-growth gurus tell you
growth will never happen because of your location; regardless if
you are in a rural setting or an urban setting; regardless if you are
in a transitional neighborhood, economically, socially, or racially,
or in a nontransitional neighborhood—Jesus is still in the business of taking little and doing much for the kingdom of God.

It is my hope that this book can help move you from the
notion that you must be a "megachurch" to do ministry. The
belief that a church has to be "mega" to do ministry is a belief
that Jesus can't do miracles in the life of the present-day church.
Although megachurches seem to have all the resources to do
ministry, this does not disqualify small to midsize churches from
engaging in effective ministry. No longer can the church use the

cop-out statement "We can't do that because we are too small." I resent that statement because it implies, in my opinion, that God can't use us for ministry until we are "mega." No, I don't like that statement, and no longer should we think in such a way.

No longer should the church dwell in maintenance mode, simply surviving from year to year and considering that a goal. No longer can the church be dictated by the church budget, always asking how much will it cost; rather, the budget should be dictated by the ministry needs of the church. No longer can the church be bound to the past, always using the words "We've never done it that way before." If Jesus can take little and do much in the feeding of the five thousand, Jesus can take little and do much in the life of the church today, regardless of the size. If God can breathe new life as God did in the story of the valley of dry bones in the book of Ezekiel, God can breathe new life into our churches today, regardless of the size.

Having said all that, I must note, I learned these lessons "going up the rough side of the mountain." Although Dellrose has grown to a membership of more than 600, and vitality can be seen throughout the church today, there was some pain that came with the journey (I wish I knew then what I know now!). There was the pain of feeling I was all by myself with no resources. How I would have appreciated some help along the way! But as one writer has stated, and I agree, "I won't take nothing for my journey." For on this journey I learned that Jesus could take an ineffective church and make it effective. Jesus can take little and do much with those who believe.

Believe in what, you ask? Believe that if a church is healthy, regardless of size, it will produce growth! There is pain that comes with transforming a declining, dying church to a vital, healthy church. If Dellrose United Methodist Church was to overcome a slow institutional death, this painful question had to be asked: How do you revitalize an ineffective, nonsustainable, and dying church so it becomes an effective, sustainable, vital, and healthy church?

Statistics indicate the mainline church is on a downward spiral with a graying membership, declining rolls, in neighborhoods transitioning economically and culturally, and in the grasp of institutional death where ministry is noneffective. How do you beat the statistics?

Regardless of the size of the church, if it is not healthy it will die; and I believe anything dead ought to be buried. As painful as this may sound, it is the only process by which new birth can begin. If an ineffective, nonsustainable, nonvital church implements an aggressive process of measurable and effective church leadership and administration, the results will be an increase in key congregational indicators—worship, discipleship, and ministry—and the church will become effective, sustainable, and vital. My personal slogan is: "Reach the lost, teach the found, and send the taught." I believe every church should focus on these three things: first, reaching the lost; second, teaching the found; and third, sending the taught. If we are faithful in these three, God will take little and do much in worship, discipleship, and ministry, regardless of the size of our budget or the number of members on our rolls.

Biblical Foundation

The inspiration for Dellrose's new birth is found in the book of Ezekiel. In Ezekiel 37, the Spirit of God leads the prophet into a valley of dry bones, the bones that represented life from another time. God asks a very powerful question of Ezekiel: "Mortal, can these bones live?" (Ezekiel 37:3).

In other words, God is asking Ezekiel, "Can there be life again, where there is no vitality, or sustainability, but only death and decay?" Is revitalization possible; can an ineffective church be transformed into a vital, healthy congregation? In the book of Ezekiel, chapter 37 verses 1-10 states:

> The hand of the LORD came upon me, and he brought me out by the spirit of the LORD and set me down in the middle of a valley; it was full of bones. He led me all around them; there were very many lying in the valley, and they were very dry. He

said to me, "Mortal, can these bones live?" I answered, "O Lord GOD, you know." Then he said to me, "Prophesy to these bones, and say to them: O dry bones, hear the word of the LORD. Thus says the Lord GOD to these bones: I will cause breath to enter you, and you shall live. I will lay sinews on you, and will cause flesh to come upon you, and cover you with skin, and put breath in you, and you shall live; and you shall know that I am the LORD." So I prophesied as I had been commanded; and as I prophesied, suddenly there was a noise, a rattling, and the bones came together, bone to its bone. I looked, and there were sinews on them, and flesh had come upon them, and skin had covered them; but there was no breath in them. Then he said to me, "Prophesy to the breath, prophesy, mortal, and say to the breath: Thus says the Lord GOD: Come from the four winds, O breath, and breathe upon these slain, that they may live." I prophesied as he commanded me, and the breath came into them, and they lived, and stood on their feet, a vast multitude.

This text is a perfect example of how God is speaking about revitalization and how an ineffective context can become an effective context. However, only the Spirit of God working through God's people can do this transformation and revitalization. One person God used to revitalize the children of Israel was Ezekiel. God commands Ezekiel to prophesy to the dry bones in the valley.

With Ezekiel prophesying to the dry bones, the dry bones heard the word of God and through that hearing, the breath of God gave the people of God new life. "God [caused] 'breath' or 'spirit' to enter them, and they lived" again.[1] The purpose of the Spirit of God in this passage of text is to remind the people that revitalization can take place only by the Spirit of God. The church cannot revitalize itself: "Not by might, nor by power, but by my spirit, says the LORD of hosts" (Zechariah 4:6b). And if the church attempts to revitalize without the Spirit of God, the church will soon discover "unless the LORD builds the house, those who build it labor in vain" (Psalm 127:1a). Therefore, in order to revitalize an ineffective, nonsustainable, and nonvital church, the church must first allow God's Spirit to enter and permeate the church.

The Fourfold Process

This . . . will be accomplished through a fourfold process [found in the story of the valley of the dry bones].

First, God will lay sinews upon them, binding bone to bone. Second, [God] will cause flesh to come upon them. Third, skin will cover the flesh. This sequencing of events reverses the process by which bodies decompose. Finally, God will infuse them with breath (or "spirit"). As a consequence of these procedures, the bones will live; more importantly, the Lord's larger purpose will be accomplished: the revived people will know and acknowledge who [God] is.[2]

When reading Ezekiel, God breathes on the whole body of dry bones. Note, when God breathed on the whole body through the prophecy of Ezekiel, "suddenly there was a noise, a rattling, and the bones came together, bone to its bone . . . And there were sinews on them, and flesh had come upon them, and skin had covered them . . . I prophesied as he commanded me, and the breath came into them, and they lived, and stood on their feet, a vast multitude" (Ezekiel 37:7-10).

It is clear from this passage: first, in order for an ineffective church to become an effective church, it will need leadership and administration such as Ezekiel who will prophesy life into the body of the congregation. By prophesying life where there is no life, God can take what was dead and bring life; God can take little and turn it into much. By prophesying/preaching to the body, allowing the body to hear the word of the Lord, the body comes together, uniting bone to bone, transforming from death to life, standing on its own feet, a vast multitude: vital, healthy, sustainable, and effective.

Once God breathes upon the body, the Spirit of God gives direction and vision to the body. This is vital to the church because "where there is no vision the people perish" (Proverbs 29:18 KJV). *The New Revised Standard Version of the Bible* translates this same verse as "Where there is no prophecy, the people cast off restraint." Therefore, in order for an ineffective church to become an effective church, not only must the Spirit of God breathe on them, they must also be led by the Spirit of God. This includes the whole church, from head to toe; from the core to the outer; from paid staff to volunteers; from adult ministries to children's ministries; from nurturing ministries to outreach ministries.

It Takes Teamwork

To do this and to revitalize an ineffective, nonsustainable church, teamwork is essential to the vitality and life of the church. One person cannot do it all. The pastor of the church should not attempt to do all the work in the church. When God spoke to Ezekiel, God spoke to Ezekiel only about prophesying to the dead bones. God did not give Ezekiel all the work. And even today God does not give all the work to one person but gives the work of ministry to the entire body. This is also seen in the "feeding of the five thousand" (see John 6:1-14). When Jesus took the two fish and five loaves of bread, he didn't hand out the fish and bread individually to each of the five thousand people. Rather, Jesus took what was little and handed it to his disciples. The disciples in turn had the people sit in groups; once the people were in groups, the disciples gave the fish and bread to the group leaders. The group leaders in turn gave the fish and bread to the group; the entire body ate and was satisfied. What this shows is effective administrative teamwork.

Trying to do everything is not an effective method of doing ministry. God did not call us to be "Lone Ranger" ministers; rather, God has called us to be in relational ministry where God's people work together for the building up of God's kingdom here on earth.

Michael Jordan

Michael Jordan, the famous basketball player for the Chicago Bulls, knew that, though great, he could not win by himself. Michael knew it took teamwork to be effective. Michael's acknowledgment that he needed help made him even more effective on the court, and season after season the Chicago Bulls won championship after championship. Why? Because of effective teamwork. Michael may have been the star player on the team and even the centerpiece in some people's eyes. However, Michael understood that in order to be effective, he could not be the centerpiece of the puzzle; rather, he just wanted to be a piece of the championship puzzle. Teamwork!

Moses and Jethro

In the book of Exodus, we find a perfect example of teamwork and how it can help an ineffective context become an effective context:

> The next day Moses sat as judge for the people, while the people stood around him from morning until evening. When Moses' father-in-law saw all that he was doing for the people, he said, "What is this that you are doing for the people? Why do you sit alone, while all the people stand around you from morning until evening?" Moses said to his father-in-law, "Because the people come to me to inquire of God. When they have a dispute, they come to me and I decide between one person and another, and I make known to them the statutes and instructions of God." Moses' father-in-law said to him, "What you are doing is not good. You will surely wear yourself out, both you and these people with you. For the task is too heavy for you; you cannot do it alone. Now listen to me. I will give you counsel, and God be with you! You should represent the people before God, and you should bring their cases before God; teach them the statutes and instructions and make known to them the way they are to go and the things they are to do. You should also look for able men among all the people,

men who fear God, are trustworthy, and hate dishonest gain; set such men over them as officers over thousands, hundreds, fifties and tens. Let them sit as judges for the people at all times; let them bring every important case to you, but decide every minor case themselves. So it will be easier for you, and they will bear the burden with you. If you do this, and God so commands you, then you will be able to endure, and all these people will go to their home in peace." So Moses listened to his father-in-law and did all that he had said. Moses chose able men from all Israel and appointed them as heads over the people, as officers over thousands, hundreds, fifties, and tens. And they judged the people at all times; hard cases they brought to Moses, but any minor case they decided themselves. Then Moses let his father-in-law depart, and he went off to his own country. (Exodus 18:13-27)

This text has Jethro, the father-in-law of Moses, giving advice on how to do ministry effectively as a team, not as an individual. Although Moses was a leader, his administrative skills were leading him to an early death. Administratively, Moses was not effective, nor would he have been able to sustain the ministry. "We do not know whether Moses is so concerned with control that he wants to handle all the cases himself, or if he is unreflective and has never thought about a more workable, practical system."[3] Think about that first statement, of Moses being concerned about control and power. This kind of attitude will always kill a church. Not only was Moses unsure of himself, "Moses seems not to have much common sense about administrative matters."[4]

Domineering people who have poor reflective skills and lack common sense tend not to be good administrators. They burn out quickly, far before the ministry actually launches from the pad. This type of ministry is hurting and even killing thousands of churches today. From reading the text, it seems Jethro already knew what this type of ministry could do to Moses and the people of Israel.

Jethro knew that Moses had to learn quickly the art of delegation:

Jethro thus proposes a judicial system, distinct from the primitive practice of one-man adjudication. The proposal includes (a) the recruitment of good people (v. 21); (b) their training and preparation (v. 20); (c) a system of courts for different social units (v. 21); (d) a "high court" over which Moses would preside (v. 22); and (e) continued affirmation that the entire system would be referred to the will of God (vv. 19, 23).[5]

Such a system will save Moses from burnout, but more important, it will let the community go home in [shalom]—i.e., in harmony and wholeness, free of conflict, enjoying a stable, shared welfare (v. 23).[6]

Even today, the type of system Jethro advised to Moses can be a model to help noneffective, nonsustainable, and dying churches become effective, sustainable, vital, and healthy churches. Regardless of what size the church may be, when we realize that all people are a part of the body of Christ and that it is God's Spirit that connects, guides, and empowers the church to work together as a team for the will of God, we have the great joy of knowing that all churches, no matter what size, can take little and do much.

CHAPTER TWO

PASTOR AND PARISH—TWO STORIES CONVERGE

The human mind may devise many plans, but it is the purpose of the LORD that will be established. (Proverbs 19:21)

Pastor: The Start of "Real Life"

What my mother referred to as "real life" started for me on May 11, 1991. I had just graduated from the University of Texas at El Paso, Texas. Walking across the stage to receive my diploma, "real life" whispered in my ear, "What are you going to do with the rest of your life?" I quickly answered, "I'm going to use my degree in criminal justice and become a police officer, and then, later, become an FBI agent." That is what I thought I wanted to do for the rest of my life. I soon discovered that was not what God had in mind.

After graduation, I returned home to Wichita, Kansas, where I was a police officer for the Wichita Police Department for three and a half years, writing speeding tickets, chasing felons, and even praying with battered mothers and crying children. Although I enjoyed my profession, I resigned from the police department August 1995. My reason was that I was offered a full-time position in ministry at the local church I attended.

During my rookie year as a police officer, an acquaintance invited me to church. I can remember that day so well; it was in April 1992, a beautiful spring Sunday morning. As we pulled up in the parking lot, I thought my friend was playing a joke on me; it was a United Methodist church. As an African-American male who had grown up Baptist, I said to my friend, "What are you doing, bringing me to a United Methodist church?" My friend's reply: "Come on, it won't hurt to visit one of the fastest growing churches in town."

As we opened the front door and entered the narthex, I soon discovered why this church—Saint Mark United Methodist Church in Wichita, Kansas, under the leadership, at that time, of Pastor Tyrone D. Gordon—was one of the fastest growing churches in town. The music was melodies from heaven, the people were angels from heaven, and the sermon was bread from heaven; it was as if I had died and gone to heaven. I thought that there couldn't be a friendlier church. From the moment we walked in, there was a warm, welcoming spirit from all those we came in contact with. Based on my first impression of Saint Mark, I joined the church with about ten other people that same Sunday. This was a common experience for many first-time visitors. However, Saint Mark was not always the fastest growing church in town; it was once a small community church, which had morphed into a booming megachurch through the visionary leadership of its pastor, Tyrone D. Gordon.

After joining Saint Mark, my passion to serve God grew each day. This passion to serve God grew more and more as I attended midweek Bible study on Wednesday nights. It was during a Wednesday night Bible study that I finally accepted the call into ministry, which I believe I had been struggling with since the age of eighteen.

I spoke with Pastor Gordon, explained to him that I had accepted my call, and began my journey into the ministry. I soon joined the choir and even got involved in helping visitation ministry. While visiting the sick and shut-ins, the call from God to do ministry grew even more. Evidently at that time, Pastor

Gordon saw the same thing. In the summer of 1993, he invited me to serve part-time as the minister of the sick and shut-ins.

I served in this position for one year while I was still a full-time police officer. I was then invited to serve part-time as the youth minister in 1994. It was during this time as the youth minister that I completely accepted my call into the ministry; no longer could I deny the call God had on my life.

In the summer of 1995, I was invited to attend a two-week local pastor's school were I received my local pastor's license. I then received my first appointment from the Kansas West Conference to be the full-time associate pastor of Saint Mark United Methodist Church.

That same summer I resigned from the police department. Also that summer, I spoke to "real life" and said, "I now know this is the work God has called me to do." I don't think I even stopped at my spiritual fork in the road. I left the police department in full stride to answer my call to pastor. From August 1995 to August 1997, as the associate pastor of Saint Mark United Methodist Church, God was, needless to say, preparing me for Dellrose United Methodist Church, just one mile east of Saint Mark.

During the intense time at Saint Mark, learning all the practical and theoretical aspects of doing great ministry, I figured I needed to enhance my ministry for greatness theologically, so I applied for seminary. Although attending seminary is a requirement in The United Methodist Church to become an ordained clergy, I went to sharpen my gifts as a pastor for the local church. I wanted to be a great instrument for God to use in building up God's kingdom here on earth.

I received notice that I was accepted as a seminary student at Phillips Theological Seminary, located in Tulsa, Oklahoma. Although the seminary was affiliated with The Disciples of Christ Church, it was only a two-hour commute from Wichita, and a perfect fit for me at that time in my life.

The commute allowed me to continue my ministry at Saint Mark while I attended seminary. I began in January 1996. During my first semester, I soon discovered going to seminary full-time and being in ministry full-time, especially at a church that demanded full attention, could not coexist. After a year and a half I had to make a decision; during the summer of 1997, as painful as it was, I decided to resign as associate pastor of Saint Mark to devote my full attention to seminary. I made the decision believing that to be a great pastor for God to use, mediocre was not an option. When I made that decision, however, I did not know God was preparing me for a greater ministry than I could ever imagine.

But with faith in God, knowing God "will not forsake his faithful ones" (Psalm 37:28b), my wife, Teketa, assumed the primary breadwinner role as I devoted my time to three weekly commutes to seminary while working as a part-time classified teacher in the Wichita public school system. That one year as a schoolteacher taught me a valuable lesson in how to adapt to change as well as meeting people where they are. If you ever want to test your speaking skills, try teaching four classes a day four days a week to a group of sixth, seventh, and eighth graders. Here you will discover if God has truly called you to the gift of communication and preaching.

Lessons from Saint Mark

During my time at Saint Mark, I learned about the day-to-day operation of a large, growing church. I learned that every aspect of ministry should be done with a mind-set of excellence—Total Quality Ministry. No longer should ministry be done halfheartedly; rather, it should be done fanatically with an incurable need to produce results.

I must state my opinion here that this is the reason for the death of a lot of our churches today: a lack of quality ministry, a lack of enthusiasm, and a lack of vision. As long as a local church is in maintenance mode, striving only to survive, it will never achieve quality. However, if a local church strives daily—as I learned at Saint Mark as an associate pastor—for total quality ministry, for excellence, and for high standards in ministry, it will become a healthy and thriving church. No longer should churches strive to be good; rather, every church should strive to be great. As Jim Collins states in his book *Good to Great*, "Good is the enemy of great."[1] He goes on to say,

> We don't have great schools, principally because we have good schools. We don't have great government, principally because we have good government. Few people attain great lives, in large part because it is just so easy to settle for a good life. The vast majority of companies [and churches] never become great, precisely because the vast majority become quite good—and that is their main problem.[2]

At Saint Mark, I learned good was not great enough! Excellence was Great!

Parish: History of Dellrose United Methodist Church

On Monday evening, October 8, 1951, at the home of Mr. and Mrs. James Keehley Jr., a group of men and women who were interested in organizing a Methodist Church in the northeast section of Wichita, met with Dr. Robert A. Hunt, District Superintendent of the Wichita District.

....

On Sunday October 14, 1951, at 3:00 P.M., the first worship service was held in the University Methodist Church at 17th and Volutsia, with Dr. Hunt presiding and giving a very challenging message. At the end of the service 17 persons were received into membership.[3]

So began the story of Dellrose United Methodist Church. Construction on the building was started in March 1952 and completed on September 21, 1952. Dellrose's first full-time pastor was the Reverend Everett Mitchell, who was appointed

October 1952. In 1954, an addition was made to the church building, due to the growth of the congregation and its ministry to the immediately surrounding community.

On January 2, 1968, a called Quarterly Conference authorized the employment of architects for the new church building, and on July 19, 1970, the new church was completed. The membership at this time was well over 500. The members were active in the neighborhood and surrounding community and in the church doing great ministry. The 1970s and most of the 1980s were considered the heyday for Dellrose United Methodist Church, with an average attendance of 300.

In the late 1980s, a transition began to take place in the church and in the neighborhood. The church membership began to age, and the community began to transition from Anglos to African-Americans. Membership and attendance fell drastically. In the early 1970s membership was approximately 500 and attendance was approximately 300; by 1992, membership was approximately 200 and attendance was 124. The church was declining in all areas of ministry. The decline came from what I call complacency and a lack of ministry, to and with the immediately surrounding community. This led Dellrose to a valley of decay and death.

Dellrose was not alone in this decline. This story was, and is, seen throughout the entire mainline protestant church. When we pull back the veil of our transitioned communities, we discover that the churches that did not embrace the transition became valleys of dry bones. Churches that did not give in to complacency, however, were "standing on their feet, a vast multitude." As we have already seen (see page xiii), the mandate for United Methodists is provided in our *Book of Discipline*.

With the increasing change in the neighborhood, the church leaders put together a study group to see how Dellrose could effectively respond to the transition. This was a courageous step for the church. One outcome of the study was the decision—made jointly by the district superintendent, the conference leadership, and the church—to appoint an African-American pastor. This decision was based on the discovery of the study group that if Dellrose wanted to continue to thrive, it would have to alter its ministries and worship style to meet the needs of the new community.

Through the study, Dellrose realized the importance and urgency of the local congregation's response to the changes occurring in its surrounding community. Dellrose discovered they were responsible to organize its mission and ministry accordingly for transition communities.

The church's first attempt was with Reverend Moore in 1994, an African-American pastor who had planned to retire in four years. The attempt was not successful. I believe it failed because it didn't go far enough. Just changing the race of the pastor will not bring revitalization. As a matter of fact, I don't care what color or sex a pastor is, if the pastor and congregation do not have a passion and a desire to meet the needs and cultural patterns of the new residents, death is surely ready to knock at the church's door. The second attempt at transition was with me, Kevass J. Harding. In 1998, I was appointed to Dellrose United Methodist Church. When I arrived on August 5, 1998, membership was approximately 100, with an average attendance of 50.

Stories Converge

The Phone Call

Finishing another grueling day of seminary, I had just flopped down in my favorite chair in our living room when Teketa, my wife, poked her head out of the kitchen. She told me to return the call of my district superintendent of The United Methodist Church. I dragged myself into my bedroom, sat down on the edge of the bed, returned the call, and nearly dropped the phone when asked if I would accept an appointment as the pastor of Dellrose United Methodist Church. Composing myself and taking a deep breath, I crossed my legs, deepened my voice, and said I would be glad to.

Then I hung up the phone and did some flips in our living room. My wife and I were holding hands, shouting and thanking God. I was amazed at how quickly God had moved me from police work to pastor.

The district superintendent had given me a date to meet with the Pastor Parish Relations Committee for my introduction. The meeting was held the second week of February 1998; my appointment as senior pastor would start July 5, 1998.

The First Meeting

At that first meeting with the Pastor Parish Relations Committee and the district superintendent, I was advised it was time for the church to make the transition needed to minister to the surrounding neighborhood. This was based on the work the Dellrose study group did in the late 1980s and early 1990s. It was time for a significant change, and I noticed God beginning a ministry of taking little and doing much.

After the superintendent prayed, the meeting was open for discussion. As we talked, I was asked what I expected to happen when I began my pastoral appointment. I boldly declared, "I expect someone to join the church every Sunday morning." This bold declaration was embedded in my spirit by my mentor and pastor, Tyrone D. Gordon, as of this writing, the pastor of Saint Luke "Community" United Methodist Church in Dallas, Texas.

One of the committee members, with a smirk on his lips, said, "I'd like to see that."

I asked him why he would say such a thing.

He exclaimed, "We have not had one person join this church since the first of the year. What makes you think they will start now?"

I replied, "I have faith that at the end of each sermon, when we open the doors of the church and give the invitation of Christian discipleship, someone will join the church." Another great mentor, Dr. Zan Wesley Holmes Jr., the former pastor of Saint Luke "Community" United Methodist Church, implanted this belief and statement in my spirit.

The room was silent for a moment, and then the committee member's voice broke the silence: "If we are planning for transition, it would be good if someone would join every Sunday." I agreed and asked him how he supposed we would do that.

He replied, "Get out in the community and evangelize."

I again agreed, but with some concern. I asked, "Are you sure?"

I asked that question, "Are you sure," because I knew that Dellrose was a declining, predominantly white church with a graying membership surrounded by a growing, predominantly black, middle-class working community. I knew that for Dellrose to evangelize its surrounding community, the congregation would need to drastically transform its mission and ministry. I knew this transformation would call for the members to go beyond the four walls of the church and into the community itself. I soon discovered this in itself would be a great challenge.

Although I had some reservations, I accepted the appointment. I believed God was about to do a great and awesome work in the life of Dellrose. As I already shared in the introduction, my launching pad for this transitional change came from the 1996 *Book of Discipline*. It bears repeating:

> When the communities where the church is located experience transition especially identified as economic and or ethnic, the local church shall engage in deliberate analysis of the neighborhood change and alter its programs to meet the needs and cultural patterns of the new residents. The local church shall make every effort to remain in the neighborhood and develop effective ministries to those who are newcomers, whether of a cultural, economic, or ethnic group different from the original or present members.[4]

Awaking in the Valley of Dry Bones

I believed, naively, that these good church folks were hungry for change, ready to join me on a journey to faithful, effective ministry. I believed they were ready to follow the steps laid out in *The Book of Discipline*, the guidebook for our denomination, for meeting the needs and cultural patterns of the area's new residents. I was wrong! Again and again, I was surprised at the strength and passion of the opposition I encountered to new ideas:

"We cannot do that here. We aren't Saint Mark!"

"We have never done it that way before."

"That's not how we do things here."

"You are moving too fast."

"We don't have enough money/volunteers/time/energy..."

"You don't understand us."

"You don't belong here."

These folks believed I was trying to make Dellrose into a little Saint Mark. This was not true at all; I was trying to stop the church from being merely a social club, benefiting its own members, and neglecting the ministry needs of the community.

The ministry of fellowship, worship, and discipleship is critically important, but when it revolves around the same few—inside the church, Sunday after Sunday, never making an impact on the immediate community and neighborhood—it is not a church but a social club. Social club friends gather on Sunday morning for an hour of Bible study, followed by an hour of worship, and afterward return to the safety of their homes. Most of those homes, if not all, are not located in the same community or neighborhood as the church building. Churches that were once vital become complacent or fearful of the changes in the neighborhood. Members move out of the community, and the church decays into a social club. Death will soon follow.

I had entered the valley of dry bones, surrounded by decay. Dellrose was dying, and the members would not see it and would not lift a finger to change it.

My heart was so heavy, I felt I wanted to quit the ministry. Many days, I wept in pain and loneliness. Yet I believe that when I am weak God is strong. From the presence of God I received strength to go on working with this tiny, dying church.

The Megachurch Myth

A part of my strength came from a fundamental belief that God can take little and do much. So many Christians today flock to huge churches that meet every conceivable need— from childcare to singles' ministries, foreign language study to social activism—and there is nothing wrong with that. Big does not mean bad to me. I came from a big church. But neither should small mean bad. Small and midsize churches have just as important a role in God's work as does the so-called megachurch. God can take little and do much. What we have to do is overcome our own selfish desires and let the love of God shine throughout the life of the local church, regardless of whom our neighbor may be.

The Transforming Power of Possibility

With the revived strength given by God to go on, and with the support of my wife, family, new members (eventually), some colleagues (not all), my district superintendent and bishop, Dellrose has been able to overcome the challenges by altering ministries and programs to meet the needs and cultural patterns of the new residents. During this time I learned about the transforming power of possibility and wanted desperately to share it with Dellrose. I consider myself a theologian who wants to free people from constrained thinking—the kind of devilish thinking that whispers to a person's heart that they cannot do something because there are not enough members, not enough money, or because the church is too small. This is foolish thinking, and as long as any church thinks like this, it will be "like a dog that returns to its vomit" (Proverbs 26:11).

Choosing Death

The former members complained that the transition was too fast and if it did not stop, they would leave. They believed this would hurt the church financially and force us to stop the change. September 1998 marked the beginning of the exodus of these former members. Except for three households, every one of the former members withdrew, transferred, or removed their membership, leaving Dellrose to die. On the first Sunday of January 1999, the total membership was twenty-five. God, however, did not leave Dellrose to die!

Choosing Life

By the grace of God, Dellrose had to literally rebuild the entire ministry of the church. I will share the details in later chapters. Here, however, is a snapshot of some of the things we had to do to begin rebuilding.

- **Reach the Lost:** We revitalized worship and evangelized the neighborhood.
- **Teach the Found:** We restarted Sunday school with Bible study. Also, every new member who joined completed a new member orientation class. Dellrose was able to build up a core group of new leaders from the surrounding community.

  From this core group Dellrose developed its church council. From the church council we developed our nurture ministries, outreach ministries, and witness ministries. We then developed our administrative teams, which included the staff-parish relation team, the board of trustees, the finance team, and the leadership development team. With each of these teams, Dellrose produced job descriptions on how to do their ministry. We picked each person for ministry by giving a gift assessment test to find out which ministry they were equipped to do.
- **Send the Taught:** Once all the teams were in place, we had a church planning retreat. It was at the retreat that Dellrose put together its vision, mission, values, and covenant statements. Through this work, meaningful ministries for and with the community emerged.

Since the first Sunday of January 1999, through the work of transitioning Dellrose to meet the needs of the community, someone has joined Dellrose, on an average, every Sunday. The active membership has grown from 25 to more than 600 members, the attendance as grown from 63 to 400 per Sunday, the choir has grown from 4 to 45, and since 2003, Dellrose has paid its yearly apportionment to the annual conference in full. Yes, with little, God can do much. These bones can live!

CHAPTER THREE

REACHING THE LOST—REBUILDING WORSHIP

> He put a new song in my mouth, a song of praise to our
> God. Many will see and fear, and put their trust in the
> LORD. (Psalm 40:3)

Mortal, can these bones live?" (Ezekiel 37:3). This question that God asks of Ezekiel in the story of the valley of dry bones is a question of faith. God is asking Ezekiel, Do you believe I can take that which is dead and bring it back to life? Do you believe I can build up what has been torn down? Do you believe I can infuse vital ministry where there is no vitality? Is revitalization possible, and is little much in the hands of God? To that question, I say yes!

And by the power of God and by the Spirit of God, I believe God can breathe on the whole body of dry bones and "suddenly there [will be] a noise, a rattling, and the bones [will come] together, bone to its bone ... And there [will be] sinews on them, and flesh [will] come upon them, and skin [will cover] them ... I [will prophesy] as [God] commanded me, and the breath [will come] into them, and they [will live], and [stand] on their feet, a vast multitude" (Ezekiel 37:7-10).

I arrived at Dellrose believing that if God could do what God did in the book of Ezekiel, God could take the little at Dellrose and do much. God can even do it at your church if you have a passion to make disciples for Jesus Christ!

Rock the Boat

Vital worship is essential to the life or death of the local church. I believe a lot of our churches are dying because the worship experience has become dull, dead, and dry, having no meaning for everyday living. It is no longer relevant to its community or even central and essential to the life of the church.

This was certainly true at Dellrose. Sunday worship had become just one more appointment on the social calendar for the week. Also, the congregation continued to worship in a European style that had no relevance in a growing, now predominantly African-American community. In *African American Church Growth*, Dr. Carlyle Stewart says that "nothing is more reprehensible than black people apologizing to white people for black culture or culturally nuanced styles of ministry."[1]

If this church was going to be a thriving and healthy church, vital for its community, the worship experience needed to change to meet the needs of the cultural patterns of the new residents. This meant changing the worship experience.

If you are in a church that is struggling with little and feeling as if you cannot do much, I invite you to take a team of faithful leaders who are not afraid of change and investigate the possibility of getting new wineskins for new wine. Change the worship experience.

I must caution, however, there is a price to pay when you step out to change worship. You will be considered a rebel without a cause. You will be looked upon as vile, despicable, and contemptible—the evil one from hell. This is no exaggeration. Why? Most people resist change. "Church folks," especially, tend to hold on to tradition as if it were the gospel itself.

I have witnessed many leaders and pastors, who have gone into churches with a passion for ministry, choose instead to simply go along to get along; "Just give me my paycheck." Because of the deep resistance to change, they find it easier to maintain the status quo. But I dare you to rock the boat! Many of our churches that were once beacon lights of hope in our communities are fading away because of a lack of boat rockers. What do I mean by boat rockers? I mean people like Kirby Jon Caldwell, John Ed Matheson, Candace Lewis, Adam Hamilton, Rudy Rasmus, Michael Slaughter, Rose Booker-Jones, Jeff Gannon, and Junius Dotson.

I personally believe if we had more boat rockers going against the grain, not choosing to maintain the status quo, churches that sit in communities where people need healing every day would truly be hospitals for sinners and not museums for saints. If that means losing some traditional "church folks" to gain those who once were lost but now are found, let them go! Sign their transfers and wish them well!

If the church is going to be about Jesus' business of "bringing good news to the poor, proclaiming release to the captives, recovery of sight to the blind, letting the oppressed go free, and proclaiming the year of the Lord's favor" (see Luke 4:18-19); then the church with little wanting to do much must be willing to lose those "church folks" who are resistant to change, in order to be faithful to Jesus' mission of making disciples. Once I stopped apologizing and allowed Jesus to use my little faith, much began to happen. Renewal and vitality could be seen in the church.

So the first place Dellrose rocked the boat was in worship. This became clear when, prior to my first Sunday as pastor, I was invited to attend one of Dellrose's worship services.

Learning from Luther

My wife, Teketa, and I, along with our young son, Carnez, and daughter, Makayla, woke up early as usual, preparing for Sunday morning worship. As we were driving to the church, I began to wonder how much of a transition Dellrose had made as a result of the research done by the study group.

As my family and I sat in worship, I quickly discovered that what the community needed and what Dellrose offered did not, and would not, match. I sat there in the pew with a grieved spirit, knowing that what I was experiencing would not be relevant for Dellrose's surrounding community.

Worship was what I think of, from my own personal experience, as typical and traditional in a United Methodist church. I sat there feeling as if I were in the midst of a one-hour social club get-together: the sermon was a sidebar, the music was entertainment, and the children's moment was show-and-tell time. All the while my heart cried out, "Is there a balm in Gilead?" Is this church a balm of healing for the surrounding community? If not, how can it become just that, a balm in Gilead?

As these thoughts ran through my mind, I was reminded of some reading I had done in seminary. One of our reading assignments was *Spiritual Entrepreneurs: 6 Principles for Risking Renewal* by Michael Slaughter (Abingdon Press, 1995). While reading this brilliant book, I came across a quotation about Martin Luther, who had a passion to repair the vast chasm between the good news of Jesus and the culture of his time. Luther wanted so keenly to reach the people in his community that he did something "new": he set the good news of Jesus to the tunes of the popular music of his day:

> [His] tunes were largely made up of phrases from plainsong or adaptations of current songs, some of which were already associated with sacred words and some with secular. He was chided for going so far afield as to bring folk songs into the sanctuary ... And the practical effect of Luther's course was not to secularize church song so much as to turn the current of German music into a religious channel ... The twice-told tale of his phenomenal success in making popular song his agent in spreading the gospel and heartening the gospelers does not need to be repeated here.[2]

With that thought in mind, I walked out of the church after worship, looking and listening to the surrounding community. The music I heard in the Dellrose worship service and the music I heard in cars that passed by the church were totally different. In the community I heard hip-hop, R&B, rap, and even contemporary gospel music. I never heard one person playing pipe organ music in their car. This suggested to me that if I wanted to reach the masses in this community, I needed to strive with the same passion Martin Luther had. It was as if I was having my own personal moment of epiphany. In that moment the spirit of Martin Luther challenged me to be a boat rocker and go against the grain by preparing a new worship style.

First Sunday

My first Sunday as pastor of Dellrose United Methodist Church was July 5, 1998. My family and friends, and 150 members from Saint Mark United Methodist Church, came out to support me. I was excited, filled with energy and anticipation.

I didn't make any drastic changes that first Sunday. Most of the service followed a traditional United Methodist pattern. I soon discovered, however, that the sermon style and congregational participation were a drastic change for 97 percent of the current members. In the week immediately following that first Sunday, I received anonymous letters, informing me of some intense dislike for the new worship style.

I can remember some of the statements in those letters. I remember them because they pierced like daggers. Here are some examples:

"I cannot endure services like we had last Sunday—the shouting, constant amens, clapping through the service, standing up, throwing arms in the air, constant babbling, people arriving all through the service. In other words, we had constant confusion."

"It was so distracting, I could not tell you one thing that was said in the sermon."

"If I wanted that kind of service, I would be attending a Pentecostal church."

"I felt a suppressed desire to stand up and tell everyone to shut up. I'm sure you are glad I left."

"Up to the time I left, ten people had left the service."

Although those words pierced like daggers, in the same week I also received this letter—as if Christ knew I needed a refreshing reminder of his presence:

Dear Pastor, Mrs. Harding, and Family,
      I had to just write a note to say how much I enjoyed the service. It was our first. Your church, oh, what a wonderful feeling, my heart started beating so fast when I first saw you standing before us, and believe me, it never stopped beating fast. Oh, what a great feeling. Remember there will be some hills along the way, but God will always be by your side. And you can do anything. You will always be in our prayers and thoughts. May God continue to bless you and your family. Don't be too surprised if you look up and see us any day. God bless.

The Great Exodus (or the Moment of Truth)

I can safely say that I never had a honeymoon period at Dellrose—that time after arriving when everyone gets along for at least the first year. No, in the weeks following that first Sunday, I was asked to leave. If I didn't go, some of the members threatened to leave themselves, believing the church could not survive

without them. Eventually, I spoke with the district superintendent and explained that although some of the members
complained about the changes in worship, people were slowly
joining the church. Needless to say, my appointment as pastor of
Dellrose was not terminated. The realization of that fact, that I
would not be replaced, marked the moment of true transition.
Within four months, all but three families of the original members had left the church, leaving Dellrose with a total of twenty-
five members.

I called a special meeting with the remaining members at our
first, makeshift, church council meeting. This was the second
Tuesday of January in 1999. At this meeting I began to proclaim
that with God, "little is much," and to be great in the sight of
God we did not have to be a megachurch. All we needed was a
faith in God and a passion to make disciples of Jesus Christ. I pro-
claimed we would be a church that would stare death in the face
and declare we would not go to the grave; rather, we would live.

Rebuilding Worship

Now Dellrose truly began to rebuild its worship. Although
membership was small, only 25 good people, Sunday morning
attendance averaged 100 for the first six months of 1999. The
attendance helped the Sunday morning offering, which, in
turn, enabled us to hire several part-time musicians and a part-
time minister of music. One of the most outstanding and visi-
ble expressions of any worship experience is the ministry of
music. Because we believed this ministry would help us
attract guests, this was the first phase of revitalizing worship
and ministry at Dellrose.

Although we started small, the energy from the band and the
choir attracted more people to the ministry. We developed a worship team that included representatives from all areas of worship:
senior pastor; minister of music, dance, and drama; usher board;
hospitality and greeting team; media and sound system team;

communion steward team; decoration coordinator; and acolyte coordinator. We developed a nontraditional worship celebration, and people from the surrounding community began to visit and even join the church.

Our worship generally runs one hour and a half, although we don't watch the clock, and the celebrations are filled with praise and energy:

- The worship experience starts with a worship leader standing in the pulpit. As the worship leader stands in the pulpit, he or she declares, "Oh, magnify the Lord with me and let us exalt his name together."

- As the congregation stands to their feet, giving God praise, the choir processes into the worship center, marching to the choir stand.

- Once the choir is in position, they sing an opening song full of energy, excitement, and enthusiasm.

- Immediately the praise team takes over and leads the congregation in a time of praise and worship. Praise and worship is a time people are true participants, not just spectators.

- Next, a lay minister leads the church in a time of prayer.

- After prayer, we have three brief short announcements that are important for that particular week. All other announcements are read on our own time at home. Sunday morning worship is about getting in touch with God and discovering who God is in our lives, not about announcements.

- Greetings come next. We greet our guests with a song and the right hand of fellowship, as we hand out our signature candy roses.

- Immediately we move into reading the morning scripture.

- After the morning scripture, the choir sings a song of response.

- We then give our tithes and offerings.

- And the choir sings again.

- Now the preacher proclaims the Word.

- An altar call follows the proclamation of God's Word. The doors of the church are opened for people to come in response.

- After the altar call, we have a benediction.

This change didn't happen all at once. After the "great exodus" of the former members, I found myself doing everything in worship—even attempting to sing solos. I remember one particular Sunday I was singing "Amazing Grace." I thought I was doing a pretty good job until I heard the minister of music helping me with the song. She was helping by singing the song louder than I was. After worship she stated, "I like the passion you have to sing, but Pastor, you sure do need singing lessons."

Reaching the Lost in the Community

Though those first changes were painful, they helped us build a foundation of vital worship. Our goal was for worship to be relevant, intentionally designed to attract the surrounding community in which Dellrose resided. We wanted our worship experience to be so engaging that church members would invite others to the worship experience.

Keep in mind, our target area was our immediate community. We were striving to reach those who had no church home. We had an upbeat, contemporary radio ad, and a weekly newspaper ad. We bought a new sign for the front of the church and posted a new saying each week. We even put together a team of individuals to find out who lived in our neighborhood.

At first, the team consisted of my wife, my two kids, and me. This truly made me feel good. Not only was I doing ministry, my entire household was involved. Eventually our church youth joined the team. Whenever we needed to get something out in the community, it became a ministry of the youth. Although some of the doors we knocked on didn't welcome us, we continued to knock, believing that those who endure win the race. We believed this ministry of finding out who lived in our neighborhood would help us better prepare our worship celebration at Dellrose.

We walked throughout the neighborhood, week after week, inviting people to Dellrose. Besides going door-to-door, if I had an opportunity, wherever I was in the community, I invited whomever I came in contact with to experience worship at Dellrose.

One day, as I was walking and canvassing the neighborhood, I knocked on the door of a home. A woman, a single parent who looked like she was in her late twenties, opened the door. I began to introduce myself as the pastor of Dellrose United Methodist Church and, as I was speaking, she interrupted and asked very politely, "Where is Dellrose United Methodist Church?"

I replied, "Lean out your front door; you live four houses down from the church."

During my conversation with this single parent of two children, I fully realized that when a church is no longer relevant in its community, we participate in a great act of sin. Sin is missing the mark, not reaching those whom God has called the local church to minister to. I am happy to say that, after several visits to Dellrose's worship celebrations, this woman joined the church.

Though this story ends with the joy of making another disciple of Jesus Christ, I cannot help but wonder how many congregations throughout America are attempting to simply hold their own—doing what they have always done with a slowly dwindling membership. All the while there are people in the community needing and searching for a balm in Gilead; needing to hear a word from the Lord through proclamation and praise; needing to worship!

My prayer is that the people of Dellrose Church, although once few, will continue to let God do much with and through them.

My prayer is also to the readers of this book. I pray that you will have boldness and a courageous spirit to take on the intense work of rebirthing your church, preparing for new ministries, rebuilding your worship experience, and integrating newcomers into the life of your church.

> Congregational change fundamentally involves welcoming and incorporating new people. As new people arrive, they need to be both welcomed and invited to the table of food, tables of ritual, and tables of decision making. Real change happens when the disciplines of hospitality extend far beyond the front door, establishing ways to move newcomers in the shared experiences of the congregation.[3]

Led by the Spirit of God

I believe revitalization begins in the worship experience. Through worship we can help people who may believe they are just ordinary discover they are extraordinary. Let's look again at Ezekiel 37. Here we find an ordinary prophet named Ezekiel having an extraordinary worship experience.

Why do I suggest that Ezekiel is in the midst of a worship experience? First, verse 1; the Spirit of God is leading him. When the Spirit is leading us, we are in a state of worship, we can do extraordinary ministries, we can take little and do much.

When we are led by God during worship, we discover "God did not give us a spirit of [fear], but rather a spirit of power and of love and of self-discipline" (2 Timothy 1:7).

35

When we are led by the Spirit of God, we discover that "[we] can do all things through him who strengthens [us]" (Philippians 4:13).

When we are led by the Spirit of God, we can boldly say, "I am confident of this, that the one who began a good work among [us] will bring it to completion" (Philippians 1:6).

When we are led by the Spirit of God, we can "say to this mountain, 'Move from here to there,' and it will move" (Matthew 17:20).

Through the rebirthing of the worship experience at Dellrose, I have discovered that when we are led by the Spirit of God, extraordinary things happen. When ordinary people allow the Spirit of God to lead them, some extraordinary things happen in their lives:

Come here, **Moses** . . . led by the Spirit of God . . . said, "Let my people go" . . . and led the people through the Red Sea (see Exodus 3–14).

Come here, **Nehemiah,** a cupbearer . . . led by the Spirit of God . . . said to the king, "If it pleases the king . . . send me to Judah, to the city of my ancestors' graves, so that I may rebuild it" (Nehemiah 2:5).

Come here, **Gideon** . . . led by the Spirit of God . . . cut down 32,000 troops to 300 and still won the battle (see Judges 7:1-7).

Isn't it something how, when the Spirit of God is leading us, not even those in authority can stop what God wants to happen?

Let me give one more example from my own experience. In the fall of 1997, even before the call from my district superintendent, I was asleep in bed when God first showed me Dellrose Church. I woke up and told my wife, "We are going to Dellrose." Led by the Spirit of God, I would go to Dellrose and pray and worship God for whatever God was about to do. Simply put, when the Spirit of God leads us, we should expect extraordinary things to happen.

Once we have entered into worship, being led by the Spirit of God, we need to be prepared for the second part of the journey of rebirth in worship, tarrying in the valley. In 37:2, Ezekiel tells us that God "led [him] all around [the bones]; there were very many lying in the valley, and they were very dry." Regardless of how many obstacles and challenges stand in our way, we must not be overwhelmed or distracted by them.

That brings us to the third point about rebirthing worship in a dying church. Once we have entered into worship, led by the Spirit of God, and made to tarry in the valley, we are called to prophesy to the bones in season and out of season (see verses 4-5). This piece is very important for pastors striving to revitalize and infuse life into a nonvital and unhealthy church. God reminds us not to get hung up in trying to please or fix the bones; rather, we need only speak life to the bones. This is why worship is the most important aspect of taking little and doing much. It doesn't matter how many bones there are or how dry they may be. When we prophesy, when we speak life through authentic, vital worship, led by the Spirit of God, extraordinary things begin to happen in the midst of worship and in the life of the church.

Verse 7 says, "So I prophesied as I had been commanded; and as I prophesied, suddenly there was a noise, a rattling, and the bones came together, bone to its bone." When we are faithful to God's call, even in the valley of dry bones, even in a dying church, God will bring new life. Extraordinary things will happen: "I prophesied as [God] commanded me, and the breath came into them, and they lived, and stood on their feet, a vast multitude" (verse 10).

Dellrose was led by the Spirit of God to tarry in the valley. Prophesying the word of God, even after going through some hell, has had extraordinary results. Since that first worship celebration in 1998, someone has joined the Dellrose Church almost every Sunday. The active membership has grown from 25 to more than 600. Average attendance has grown from 63 to well over 350 each Sunday. The average weekly budget has grown from $1,000 to more than $5,000. Little can become much in the hands of God. These bones live again.

CHAPTER FOUR

TEACHING THE FOUND—REBUILDING DISCIPLESHIP

Go therefore and make disciples of all nations, baptizing
them . . . and teaching them. (Matthew 28:19-20)

A nnouncement! Announcement! Starting next week, Sunday school will begin every morning at 9:00 A.M." I figured if church started at 10:30 A.M., Sunday school could start an hour and a half before worship.

Although there were Sunday school classes before I arrived at Dellrose, we had to start over from scratch due to the "great exodus." All of the teachers were among the members who left. In a way, it was a blessing. By starting over from scratch, we were able to establish, not only an adult Sunday school class, but we also began classes for children and youth.

Once worship attendance and membership began to grow, I learned that the second place for rebuilding and making disciples was through Bible study. There are several ways to offer Bible studies—weekday classes, home gatherings, cell groups—but I chose Sunday school as our launching pad for discipleship.

I chose Sunday school because, quite frankly, we didn't have enough people for multiple Bible study groups. The main reason, however, was my driving passion that all who joined Dellrose would be more than just members; they would be disciples. This passion came from the biblical great commission:

"Go therefore and make disciples of all nations, baptizing them in the name of the Father and of the Son and of the Holy Spirit, and teaching them to obey everything that I have commanded you. And remember, I am with you always, to the end of the age" (Matthew 28:19-20).

I truly believe the goal of every church, regardless of size, is to make sure all of its members have an opportunity to grow spiritually and to become like Christ, to be Jesus' disciples. From that passion of wanting to make disciples, I started a Sunday morning Bible study class with just myself, my wife, and five other members. Three of them were among the few original members who had stayed. They are still members today. Although the class was small, I believed God could and would take our little class and do much with us, if we remained faithful.

And it worked. Sunday after Sunday, little by little, the class began to grow. And as we grew I could hear Paul, in the letter to the Ephesians, saying, "Equip the saints for the work of ministry, for building up the body of Christ" (4:12). Those who attended Sunday school began to grow spiritually. The growth was not automatic or instant, but it was a Sunday-by-Sunday commitment to spiritual growth.

I truly believe that some people think just because they are members of a church, they have arrived spiritually. That is a lie straight from hell. There are churches across this country filled with people who have been members all their lives, attending worship every week, and yet are spiritually empty. With that in mind, as the pastor of Dellrose, I was determined that people who joined and became members would not simply grow older in the church but would grow up spiritually. I want every member who joins the church to become like Christ. I know this is a big task. But I also know that with faith—even faith as small as a mustard seed—in the big hands of God, all this is possible.

Some people may say they already know the Bible and don't need to go to Sunday school. I say, on the contrary, spiritual growth and discipleship are not what you know but how you live and behave. It's a lifestyle, and you never stop learning how to be a disciple of Jesus Christ. I call this a commitment—a commitment to purposefully developing a relationship with Jesus Christ. Knowing the Bible is not discipleship; living the Bible is discipleship. I know many people who claim to know the Bible and can quote scripture, yet they are selfish, self-seeking, and carnal to the core of their very being; discipleship is the last thing on their minds. "Even the demons believe—and shudder" (James 2:19), and yet they are not disciples of Jesus Christ and will never be.

A Passion for Making Disciples

My passion to make disciples was greatly affected by a book titled *Working the Angles,* by Eugene H. Peterson. Peterson states, "American pastors are abandoning their posts . . . They are not leaving their churches and getting other jobs . . . But they are abandoning their posts, their *calling.* They have gone whoring after other gods."[1] He goes on to say, "Pastors of America have metamorphosed into a company of shopkeepers, and the shops they keep are churches. They are preoccupied with shopkeeper's concerns—how to keep the customers happy, how to lure customers away from competitors down the street, how to package the goods so that the customers will lay out more money."[2]

God has not called us to be shopkeepers; God has called pastors, empowering the laity, to make disciples of Jesus Christ.

> The biblical fact is that there are no successful churches. There are, instead, communities of sinners, gathered before God week after week in towns and villages all over the world. The Holy Spirit gathers them and does his work in them. In these communities of sinners, one of the sinners is called pastor and given a designated responsibility in the community. The pastor's responsibility is to keep the community attentive to God.[3]

Keeping the Community
Attentive to God

There it was. It is the pastor's responsibility to keep the community—the church—attentive to God. I read those words in the process of rebuilding Dellrose, and I committed myself to making disciples of Jesus Christ. Everything else—the numeric or financial growth of the church—would be a by-product of keeping the main thing the main thing. What was the main thing? Make disciples of Jesus Christ so that all would be attentive to God. I believe that when a person is attentive to God, they will desire to grow and be more like Christ, live like Christ, walk like Christ, talk like Christ, and love like Christ; in other words, become a disciple of Christ. Philippians 2:5 says it this way: "Let the same mind be in you that was in Christ Jesus." This literally means be like Christ, follow Christ, be apprenticed to Christ, give allegiance to Christ, and commit ourselves to Christ. Through discipleship, we put on the same mind as Christ. When we put on the mind of Christ, we become spiritually mature.

Unfortunately, many Christians attend worship only on Sunday and never move to the point of discipleship. They grow old in the church but never grow up spiritually. Because the pastor or the church leadership has not kept the community attentive to God, we have many people of all ages—20, 30, 40, 50, 60 years old, and even older—still not weaned from spiritual milk.

With deep passion I can honestly say that I do not strive to make Dellrose a megachurch. I strive to make Dellrose a disciple-making school, and if Dellrose grows into a megachurch, to God be the glory! If a church—regardless of its size, location, or finances—truly devotes its energy to making disciples first rather than making members, little will eventually become much. Even dry bones will live. I have personally discovered that members will soon leave, but disciples will stay and even multiply.

A Change in Strategy

Let me illustrate. In the first couple of years at Dellrose, I was out in the community on foot and by car, inviting any and all I could to come to our worship celebration on Sunday mornings. Every day of the week I was inviting people. And every week worship attendance and membership grew. In fact, we realized that someone was joining the church every Sunday. I was excited! We were using the marketing strategy of the fast-food franchise, and it was working. By that I mean we focused on getting people in the door and giving them filling, appealing spiritual food on Sunday mornings.

What I did not know was that most restaurants that start out fast close within a year. This soon became evident at Dellrose, too. Even though people joined the church as full members at an alarming rate the first couple of years, they soon faded away. They would join, come for about a month, full of enthusiasm, excited about doing ministry, and then disappear. They would just up and leave with no explanation. And when I saw them out in the community, they gave no reason for leaving, although they did assure me it never had anything to do with me personally.

I soon came to the conclusion that if Dellrose didn't do something quickly, we would be one more statistic, like those fast-food franchises that close within a year. We had to do more than just get the people in; we had to build them up. That building process began with discipleship. No longer would we strive for members; rather, we would strive for discipleship. Membership would be a by-product of making disciples of Jesus Christ.

No Apologies

Stating that membership would be a by-product of making disciples does not mean I'm not focused on worship. As a matter of fact, worship is the entry point for making disciples of Jesus Christ. When I first arrived at Dellrose, I used worship as a tool to get people to join the church so that the membership roll would look impressive. Now I use worship as a beginning point for making disciples. Worship is first, reaching the lost; discipleship is second, teaching the found; and ministry is third, sending the taught.

Worship is our first contact with people. During worship, a person begins to build community and becomes attentive to God. And during this time of building community, the church should—without any apology—recommend that every person who joins the church get involved in Sunday school, a small group, or a weekly Bible study. I have seen miracles happen in people's lives, families, and marriages when they moved beyond the Sunday morning experience.

If you desire to see growth in your church, I challenge you to make disciples of Jesus Christ, not members for the church. When a church, regardless of size or location, reaches, teaches, and sends, striving to make disciples of Jesus Christ, it will do much for those who join the church, for the immediate community, and even for the world.

It Started with Sunday School

And so, I made my announcement and we began Sunday morning Bible study. Little by little, our Sunday school classes grew. In fact, demand for Bible study grew to the point that we had to start classes through the week. We were able to do this because other gifted teachers emerged.

On Sunday morning we had three classes: one for children, one for youth, and one for adults. The next class was a midweek Bible study class on Wednesday nights. Because we had gifted teachers for Sunday morning, I taught the Wednesday night class. As we continued to grow we started a men's Bible study and a women's Bible study. Both of those classes are held on Monday nights. We also have a children's Bible study class on Tuesday nights along with a youth Bible study class.

Through these classes, the membership of the church grew to desire a deeper understanding of the Word of God, and we began DISCIPLE, a thirty-four-week Bible study. We started the DISCIPLE class in the fall of 2002. It was even recommended and approved that all leaders of the church complete the course.

Today, Dellrose has a total of seven DISCIPLE classes, including one on Sunday morning for those who cannot attend through the week. Dellrose also offers and teaches a DISCIPLE class at our local prison. We hope to help those who are released from prison to have a connection with a local church.

While the Bible study classes were growing, we also put together a New Member Orientation Class. This class invites and informs new members about our congregation and The United Methodist Church as a whole. The class is held on the third Saturday of each month from 10:00 A.M. to 2:00 P.M., and we serve a light lunch. Each student in the class receives a new member orientation handbook. The handbook is a vital instrument to help new members understand their new church. During one of the sessions, the new members are given a gift assessment to reveal where God can and will use them for ministry in the life of the church. It is vital for a healthy church to assist members in discerning and following God's calling for their lives.

Invited into Relationship with Jesus

By focusing on discipleship over membership, we invite those who join to follow Jesus. In accepting this invitation, living in relationship with Jesus, a person begins to transform. As this transformation continues, that person begins to understand community, a community in which Jesus invites all to participate. We participate in a ministry of building relationships that grow together in the understanding and knowledge of God, and together we begin to understand what God would have us to do in order to fulfill the ministry to which God has called us. When Dellrose moved from striving for members to making disciples, the small seed of faith not only began to grow, but sustainability increased, and little became much.

The little became much because each new member who joined and moved toward discipleship was first invited into a relationship with Jesus Christ. It was in the relationship between Jesus Christ and the person that the individual began to understand his or her purpose and passion for ministry. Then, and only then, the person was invited to join the work of a ministry committee or team matched with that passion and purpose.

To use the imagery from Ezekiel, first we prophesy and speak life to the bones in worship. Then, with God's help, we encourage and nourish the movement of bone to bone—through Bible study and deepening commitment to community—and we see sinew and flesh come upon the bones, and skin cover them. Then, through deeper relationship with Jesus, breath enters the bones and they live and stand on their feet, ready to live the life of faithful discipleship in ministry with the community and to the world.

Story of Debi Childers

In order to understand how God can take little and do much in the lives of those who strive for discipleship and a personal relationship with Jesus Christ at Dellrose, and to understand the process of reaching, teaching, and sending, I would like to share a story about a woman named Debi Childers.[4]

Debi Childers fled from her former church, where she felt condemned. Although Debi grew up in a church, under the tutelage of her grandmother, where vacation Bible school, Sunday school, and holiday pageants were required, she also experienced condemnation and rejection. Because of that, anytime a Christian invited Debi to attend church, she would roll her eyes and state, "The last time I went to church, other than for a wedding or a funeral, my former pastor publicly reprimanded and scolded me for infrequent visits. I'll never go to another church!" While that was what she said, there was a deeper hurt behind the words. Her pastor reprimanded her for infrequent visits. The reason for those infrequent visits was the judgment and condemnation she had experienced since becoming an unwed mother at age fifteen.

Debi's face warmed with embarrassment as she told her story. Feeling totally rejected by the church, Debi said that by middle school she had started looking for friendship in the wrong crowd. In 1972, after graduating from high school, she started going to clubs and toying with drugs and alcohol. She settled down by her late twenties, but became a loner, especially in matters of faith.

Debi got a job in 1981 as a parking control checker with the Wichita Police Department. Eventually she became the office administrator for the East Patrol Station for the WPD, where I was a rookie police officer. I always read the Bible in my free time at work. I would lay hands on my police car and ask God for protection before going on patrol. Without knowing it, I was witnessing to Debi about my faith.

I invited Debi to church a few times, but she always deflected my invitation. Although I left the police department to follow my call into ministry, I never stopped extending the invitation. For years, Debi would decline. She would not accept until, in her own words, she "hit rock bottom." Caring for a blind uncle at home sapped all of her energy. She told me she felt as if she "just existed."

When I became senior pastor of Dellrose United Methodist Church, I went by the police department to invite Debi to church once again.

As I spoke to her, tears poured out as years of pent-up frustrations were released. As she wept, I said, "You need to be spiritually filled. You don't need religion; you need a relationship with Jesus Christ." Evidently those were the right words at the right time; Debi accepted my invitation. I assured her that Dellrose was not like the church from her past; we would not condemn her, but we would reconcile her.

As Debi tells the story of that first Sunday, she worried that all she had in her closet was a denim jumper. There was no time to make it to the beauty shop. So, she put on the jumper, pulled her hair back, took a deep breath, and sat in the back pew. Warm smiles, casual dress, and the Holy Spirit, she said, erased her worries. Not once did she check her watch. The following Sunday, God's presence seemed to make her glide down to the altar. She states, "The welcoming, the love, the people smiling at you. I said, 'I'm going to join. I need to change my life.'" Debi joined Dellrose Church on May 19, 1999, and began her walk with Jesus as his disciple.

A few Sundays later, she was baptized. She invited everyone she knew to witness her past being washed away. Today, everyone in the congregation knows that Debi's spot is on the front row, left side, nearest the pulpit.

Debi is not only a faithful member of the church who attends worship every Sunday, she is also a disciple of Jesus Christ. Debi started her journey of discipleship during Sunday morning Bible study. She was one of the five members of that first Sunday school class. Debi is presently an enthusiastic member of a small group engaged in DISCIPLE: UNDER THE TREE OF LIFE (DISCIPLE IV).

Not only is Debi faithful to worship and discipleship; she is also faithful to her call to ministry. In August 2005, after Debi retired from the Wichita Police Department, Dellrose hired her as our full-time office administrator. Praise the Lord!

Debi's new life includes sacrifice, she says, but it is "a sacrifice of love to my Lord and Savior Jesus Christ." Sundays used to be for shopping, mowing the lawn, or weeding her flowerbed. Today, she says, her yard is in shambles, but her soul is at peace.

Gone is the isolation from family and friends. For many years, her grandmother prayed and fasted for this change, and she got to see it before her death in 2002 at age ninety-three.

Debi says, "I've made a transformation for the better. I stopped thinking of myself and having those pity parties. I still struggle, but I know God is always there." By the way, Debi's child is a student at Phillips Theological Seminary as one of Dellrose's ministers in training. My prayer is that she will one day be appointed to Dellrose as associate pastor.

Debi's story is a true testament of reaching, teaching, and sending. When churches (regardless of size) strive to reach, teach, and send, the church can turn the world upside down and then right side up, taking little and doing much.

There are many more stories of discipleship like Debi's from the Dellrose Church community. For example: Les Smith, who had stopped going to church for nearly the same reasons as Debi, is now our youth minister, youth usher board coordinator, and a member of the choir. Les was a member of the very first *DISCIPLE: BECOMING DISCIPLES THROUGH BIBLE STUDY (DISCIPLE I)* class and part of the first graduating *DISCIPLE IV* class. Les states, "I'm so glad to be at this church. It has truly blessed my life; no, turned my life around."[5]

Carol Wertz, one of the original members who didn't leave when I became the pastor of Dellrose, never participated in any ministry prior to the transition. Carol is now our part-time business administrator. She takes care of all the financial business of the church under the supervision of the finance team. She was also a member of the first *DISCIPLE I* class and the first class of *DISCIPLE IV* graduates.[6]

The list of members of Dellrose who are now disciples of Jesus Christ is so long that I would need to write a whole book only to tell their stories.

Hopefully, from these few examples you will understand that little will become much when we strive first for relationship and community through worship and discipleship. It is my sincere hope that I have helped to deconstruct the myth that a church must become "mega" in order to achieve great ministry for God. If we just build relationship and community, keeping God as our center, growth will supernaturally occur in the transformed lives and ministry of individuals and the faithful community of disciples.

Building Community as Jesus Did

As we have already seen, in order to take little and do much— in order for dry bones to live again—a church must build community. Stephen A. Macchia lists tactics for building community in his book *Becoming a Healthy Church*. Robert Coleman first identified the list of eight tactics in the classic book *The Master Plan of Evangelism*. According to Macchia:

> Robert Coleman . . . describes in-depth the community building tactics of Jesus. Coleman summarizes the example of Jesus in eight key concepts:
>
> 1. *Selection*—Jesus called a few men to follow him who could bear witness to his life and carry on his work after he returned to the Father;
>
> 2. *Association*—he stayed with them, making it a practice to be with them, drawing them close to himself;
>
> 3. *Consecration*—he required obedience, so that they would willingly deny themselves for others;
>
> 4. *Impartation*—he gave himself away to his disciples, giving all that he had, withholding nothing, not even his own life;
>
> 5. *Demonstration*—he showed them how to live, practicing prayer, turning to the Scriptures, teaching, serving, and sharing the gospel naturally and freely;
>
> 6. *Delegation*—he assigned them meaningful work, keeping his vision before them and calling them to fulfill his will;
>
> 7. *Supervision*—he kept check on them through his questions, illustrations, warnings, and admonitions in order to keep them on course to know and fulfill his work through them;
>
> 8. *Reproduction*—he expected them to reproduce themselves in the lives of others through witness and mission.[7]

I believe that my formula of reaching, teaching, and sending parallels and complements these tactics used by Jesus. In the next chapter, we will look at this in detail as we examine the full scope of new life at Dellrose. God took little and made much. God breathed new life into dry bones, and Dellrose is now engaged in awesome ministry.

SENDING THE TAUGHT— REBUILDING MINISTRY

A disciple is not above the teacher, nor a slave above the master; it is enough for the disciple to be like the teacher, and the slave like the master. (Matthew 10:24-25)

Selection

Once worship began to grow at Dellrose, the first step in rebuilding ministry, it occurred to me that we were engaged in the selection process Jesus used. "As he walked by the Sea of Galilee, he saw two brothers, Simon, who is called Peter, and Andrew his brother, casting a net into the sea— for they were fishermen. And he said to them, 'Follow me, and I will make you fish for people'" (Matthew 4:18-19).

To clarify this point, when a church is at the beginning of transition and revitalization, the congregation must rediscover its identity. When so many of the members walked out, leaving Dellrose to die, we discovered we were actually a brand-new church, a church in its infancy. If we wanted to continue our ministry in the neighborhood, we had to be intentional about our invitation to Christian discipleship.

Our door-to-door canvassing and various advertising campaigns were effective in getting people in the door. Our lively, relevant worship and true welcome helped them believe that our invitation was sincere. As I have already said, we became good at making members, but I realized we needed to move beyond that, to making disciples.

And so, we began to employ Jesus' second tactic, association.

Association

Just as Jesus made it a practice to be with his disciples, I made it a practice to draw close to Dellrose's new members in Bible study and in fellowship, hoping that from our close association would come the longing to be disciples of Jesus Christ. Notice I have not mentioned anything about programming. My sole purpose in this was to build community within the body of Christ.

As I made it a practice to associate with the members of Dellrose, we all became intentional about reaching out to the neighborhood, rebuilding community beyond the walls of the church. Every church, regardless of size, has a responsibility to stay associated with the community in which it does ministry.

Let's Eat

One approach to helping a church build community through association, drawing people close to one another and to Christ, is through fellowship and food. As Dellrose began to grow, realizing that most people in the church were either first-time members or returning after a long time away from church, we began to offer quarterly fellowship dinners.

These dinners were, and are, a great success in building community and deepeding relationships within and beyond the church. Here is how it works: every fourth Sunday in the months of March, June, September, and December, immediately following the worship celebration, a potluck dinner is served in the fellowship hall.

The kitchen ministry is in charge of this fellowship meal. Most of the time they provide the meat (my favorite is chicken, praise the Lord!). Our guests eat first. Please understand, this meal is for everyone, but it is targeted for our first-, second-, and third-time guests who happen to be worshiping with us on that particular Sunday. This is not meant to exclude the present members. On the contrary, we hope members will come so that guests and members will have an opportunity to meet one another.

During the meal I am also able to meet and greet the people, constantly striving to build community and relationship. My prayer is that all pastors, regardless of the size of the church, will find time to meet and greet people. Jesus often took time to associate with people, often over a shared meal.

I have personally witnessed the power of association. On one particular Sunday morning, I spoke with a woman who was depressed, even suicidal. She had chosen to give church one more try, and she came to Dellrose for worship. After worship we invited her to the fellowship dinner. It was there that I spoke with her, and we were able to direct her to the help she needed for her depression.

Luke 14:13-14 states, "But when you give a banquet, invite the poor, the crippled, the lame, and the blind. And you will be blessed, because they cannot repay you, for you will be repaid at the resurrection of the righteous." When a church stays associated with the community and gives of itself, withholding nothing, God can and will bless that church, just as Jesus blessed the two fish and five loaves of bread that were able to feed more than five thousand people; a true sign of God's taking little and doing much.

Consecration and Impartation

In inviting and helping the woman just mentioned above, the members of Dellrose moved to tactics three and four—consecration and impartation. Consecration is a willingness to be obedient by denying self for others. Impartation is giving all that you have, withholding nothing, for others. This story is just one example of how God can take a little church called Dellrose and use worship to reach the lost, use discipleship to teach the found, and grow that into faithful ministry; sending the taught. Dellrose, a little church that was on the point of dying, certainly no megachurch, has been blessed tremendously in ministry—inviting the poor, the crippled, the lame, and the blind.

We have a dinner, which we call the Lord's Supper, that teaches the same principles. The woman I spoke about is now a full-time, active member of the church, all because we welcomed her and broke bread with her.

Attendance at our fellowship dinners averages just over one hundred people each quarter. (If you are in Wichita on the fourth Sunday of March, June, September, or December, don't hesitate to come by. We are located at 1502 North Dellrose, on the corner of Fourteenth and Oliver; our phone number is 316-684-5182. We promise you are always welcome to eat with us!)

Staying Focused: Demonstration

As Dellrose began to grow, I knew that in order for the church to stay healthy and vital after the transition, the church needed to keep focused on discipleship. It was time to put together a vision and mission for the church. A **vision** is like a painted picture of a car drawn by an artist. The artist comes together with a team of people. Their collective **mission** is to make the painting of the car a reality. We had to be, in essence, a visionary church, looking not only at the present but also into the future.

That future, that vision, had to be clearly seen and understood by all members. Habakkuk 2:2 states, "Then the LORD answered me and said: 'Write the vision; make it plain on tablets, so that a runner may read it.'" It also had to be real and achievable. Mission and vision are related. Here are

Dellrose's vision and mission statements, developed at our first annual retreat:

Vision Statement

Through the power of God, Dellrose will focus on being a place of empowering, equipping, teaching, and training all people regardless of who they are, so all may find strength and courage for everyday living. We will provide a place where everyone will feel the love of God, find the joy of Christ, and experience the power of the Holy Spirit.

Mission Statement

To spread the Word of God to all people and to help liberate those being challenged spiritually, physically, and mentally through dynamic teaching, fellowship, praise, and worship.

The mission is held accountable to the vision, and the vision is held accountable to God; the One who said: "Write the vision; make it plain." To keep the church accountable to both the mission and the vision, Dellrose developed a covenant statement and values statement. The **covenant** statement reminds us that we are committed to working together as a team in unity to reach God's vision for the church. The **values** statement keeps us focused on how we plan to accomplish the mission as we move toward God's vision for the church. Here are our covenant and values statements:

Covenant Statement

By the power of the Holy Spirit, Dellrose has covenanted to be a church committed to working together as a team in unity to reach God's vision for the church.

Values Statement

To keep focused on God's preferred future and on track with our mission, Dellrose will deeply value:

1. Dynamic Bible-centered preaching and teaching.

2. Excellent praise and worship.

3. Loyal giving of tithes and offerings.

4. Leaders who are committed to godly Christian service.

5. Relevant Christian education for all ages.

6. Outreaching ministries to help all people.

7. Superb fellowship so all will feel welcomed.

8. Evangelizing the Word of God throughout the community.

Therefore, we are committed to tithing as the way we support our ministry and the things that we value.

The process for writing Dellrose's vision and mission began at our first annual church retreat in February 2000. All of the members were invited to come; church leaders were required to attend. In order for God to take little and do much, God needs dedicated leadership disciples, beginning with the pastor. In Jesus' ministry, this was the tactic of demonstration: showing the disciples how to live, serve, and share the gospel.

With a desire to demonstrate our passion for how we would live, serve, and share the gospel, we worked as a team to develop our vision and mission statements. I remember that day well, the first Saturday of February. More than seventy-five members attended the first retreat. Our process began with praise and worship in song and a Bible study of Ephesians 4:1-16, using Paul's imagery of the church as the body of Christ as the foundation for our work. Here's the schedule of the day:

9:00   Registration
9:30   Welcome/Songs of Praise and Worship
9:40   Bible Study (Ephesians 4:1-16)
10:00   Community Building
10:15   Introduction of Speaker/Facilitator
10:20   Team Ministry Exercise: Getting Things Done
        Together
        1. What Is a Team?
        2. Who Are the Team Leaders?
        3. Where Does the Team Get Power?
11:30   Lunch
12:30   Songs of Praise and Worship
12:35   Teamwork starts with shared vision!
        1. What does the Scripture say? (See Proverbs 29:18.)
        2. What is God's preferred future for Dellrose?
1:40   Teamwork starts with shared mission!
        1. What does the Scripture say?
        (See Matthew 28:19-20.)
        2. What is Dellrose's reason and purpose for existing?
2:45   What Matters Most?
        (What do we value as a church?)
3:15   What Can We Covenant (as a result of today)?
3:30   Closing/Remarks

Having an outside speaker allowed me to fully participate in the retreat. Our speaker, Carolyn Anderson, brought great passion for the church and proven leadership in guiding churches to understand team, vision, and mission.

Notice that much of the day was focused on understanding team ministry. Team ministry is about being in relationship with one another. It is shared ministry. Think about how Paul describes the body of Christ in 1 Corinthians 12: the hand is important to the body, as is the foot, and the body needs both the hand and the foot—a team. The hand and the foot are in relationship with each other, sharing the ministry of helping the body see its vision and fulfill its mission of being in the image of God.

During that six-and-a-half-hour church retreat, with great discussion, we defined our vision, mission, covenant, and values statements. Carol Wertz, one of the original members who did not leave the church during the transition, stated as she left the retreat with a smile on her face, "I now know where God is leading us, and I'm ready to follow."[1]

We all agreed that these statements would be the driving force for our church. Plain and simple: if we wanted to do something that did not align with our vision and mission, we would not do it. We are so dedicated to our vision and mission that we read them aloud at the beginning of every church meeting. They are posted in the worship center and even in every office and restroom in the church.

I am proud to say that not only I, but also a majority of the church council, can recite both the vision statement and the mission statement when we meet the second Tuesday of each month for church council. With that said, I believe it is very important for the pastor to review the vision and mission statements at least once a quarter with the entire church. I often preach a sermon pertaining to our vision and mission or talk about the meaning of the words after we recite them in meetings.

From building community, expressed through our vision and mission statements, the church was organized. As we continue to organize, we look to our vision and mission to ensure that we praise God with excellence, spread the Word of God with excellence, equip the people of God with excellence, teach the people of God with excellence, and love the people of God with excellence. Using these standards, Dellrose measures its ministry once a year at our annual church retreat to make sure we are staying true to our vision and mission. By doing this, we are prepared for truly effective ministry.

Delegation

Just as Jethro understood that Moses could not do everything himself, I realized it was time to delegate. This is the sixth method Jesus used to build community. Jesus understood that ministry is not something we do by ourselves. Again, this is seen in the feeding of the five thousand, where Jesus assigned the disciples to meaningful ministry. Likewise, if a church's desire is for God to do much in the life of the church, teamwork is essential. And once the church understands the importance of delegation and teamwork, the pastor, along with the leadership team, should passionately seek the right people for the right ministry.

Do not put people into positions just to fill slots! I must state this emphatically. It will lead to all kinds of pain and frustration. When you delegate, make sure you have the right person. Do not give a person a ministry for which they have no understanding or interest. It will only lead to both of you being stressed out. Please hear this! I'm not telling you something I've heard; I'm telling you something I have experienced firsthand. If a person cannot or does not want to do a ministry, don't let them do it. For far too long, local churches have allowed either inappropriate or incompetent people the authority to run the church, and the church continues to die. Inviting people to do ministry for which they are not suited and to which they are not called does not honor or contribute to the growth of their discipleship or build up the body of Christ. Give them a gifts assessment and find their ministry gift.

Spiritual gifts are special ministries distributed throughout the membership of the church for its health and vitality and for the redemption of the world. If the body of Christ is to be all God created it to be, each member must use their gifts constantly. Every part needs to be working. Paul makes this point:

"But speaking the truth in love, we must grow up in every way into him who is the head, into Christ, from whom the whole body, joined and knitted together by every ligament with which it is equipped, as each part is working properly, promotes the body's growth in building itself up in love" (Ephesians 4:15-16).

The gifts assessment that we use is a survey of forty-five statements and questions that we call "Finding Your Place in Ministry: A Spiritual Gifts Assessment Designed to Show What You Can Do for Jesus Christ!" We believe every member needs to learn about spiritual gifts and discover how to use those gifts if the church is going to grow and build for the kingdom of God. And we believe the Lord will use the assessment to encourage members to make a commitment to a ministry that matches their spiritual gift. The gifts assessment is administered to all new members during our new member orientation class.

Supervision

Another tool that has helped me along the road, and that I believe will help every church (and again, even small churches), is job descriptions. For every position at Dellrose, paid and non-paid, there is a job description. I believe every member doing ministry should have a job description, including the senior pastor. See appendix B for some samples of our job descriptions.

Prior to hiring someone, I make sure the person understands the job description and can do the job described. "[Job] descriptions outline what an individual is to do as a part of the church organization. They define a particular piece of the church's mission, objectives, and action plans in which an individual will participate and how one is to perform."[2] The key word here is *perform*. If a person can't perform, don't hire them. I don't care if it is your mother or your best friend; don't put the church in harm's way.

What I am speaking about is Jesus' tactic of supervision, the seventh step in building community. Supervision is what keeps a church on course and makes sure ministry is on track; aligned with the vision and mission of the church.

Notice the word *supervision*. If we break it up, it becomes "super-vision." In other words, super-vision sees the big picture. If a church wants to do great things for God, its leadership—particularly the pastor—needs to see the big picture.

What is the big picture? Make disciples of Jesus Christ through ministry, discipleship, and worship. I truly believe that when a church and its leadership understand the importance of making disciples, the church will do great ministry.

Reproduction

When a church gets to the point where all three—worship, discipleship, and ministry—are working at the same time, not only will the church do great ministry, but so will each individual within the church. This is where we see reproduction happening; the last and final tactic Jesus used for building community. The church begins to reproduce itself, increasing the effectiveness and expanding the reach of faithful ministry. This takes me back once more to Ezekiel. Can these bones live? The answer is yes. With God, all things are possible.

Let me share some examples of reproduction at Dellrose. When I arrived in 1998, the church facilities were in poor shape, outdated, and in need of repair:

- Dellrose had a small, old wooden sign. Within a year and a half, we had installed a new two-thousand-dollar sign that allows us to proclaim a new message of hope to the community each week.

- The church was still using its analog telephone system from the 1970s. Today our communication system has five telephone lines with all the latest technology.

- The antiquated boiler system had to be turned on by hand, and we prayed that the air-conditioning system would be on when we came to church. Today we have a new boiler system that automatically comes on as the building needs heat, plus a new air-conditioning system that keeps the entire building cool during the summer months.

- The sound system was so old that if a person driving by used a CB radio, it interfered with worship. Today we have a state-of-the-art sound system with monitors, new speakers, soundboard, new pulpit microphones, and a handheld microphone. Along with the new sound system, Dellrose even installed sound barriers for acoustics in the worship center.

- Dellrose had no transportation to pick up those who needed a ride to and from church. Today we have a deluxe, fifteen-passenger van in which we have taken numerous trips to do ministry.

- From 25 members to 600; from 63 in worship to 400 average weekly attendance.

- Sunday school, Bible study (children, youth, and adults) now has an average weekly attendance of 150.

- Organized small-group fellowships for men, women, youth, children, couples/married, and singles.

- Outreach ministries for the entire community, including:

  - Food Bank: Staffed by a servant leader (our name for volunteers), the food bank is open Monday through Friday, 1:00 P.M. to 5:00 P.M. All food is either donated by church members or from the main food bank downtown. Every third Sunday we take up a food bank offering so we can purchase more food from the main food bank. This ministry is very important for those without transportation who live in the community immediately surrounding the church.

  - "De La Rosa" Youth Center: Through our youth center, many children in the church and in the surrounding community are able to get daily tutoring and mentoring. The center is open Monday through Friday from 3:30 P.M. to 6:30 P.M. During the summer months when children are out of school, the center is open from 8:00 A.M. to 5:00 P.M. Breakfast and lunch are served.

o Counseling center to help those who struggle with the vices of the world, open Monday through Friday by appointment only.

• Community awareness of Dellrose and ongoing efforts to keep in touch with the community.

And finally, transformed lives. Since God began to take little and do much, I have personally witnessed how God can take a person who once was hooked on drugs and make him sober and clean, able to help others to stay off drugs through our twelve-step program. God is good all the time, and all the time God is good!

Encouragement

I hope all who read this book are truly blessed. I must say, however, that this book was birthed out of the pain of not having any direction when it came to transforming a dying church. Although I received support from my annual conference and most of my colleagues, some people just did not understand (or want to understand) the task I was up against.

I shall never forget the painful exodus of members during those first three months. The pain was deepened when I reached out to a colleague whom I considered a friend, and in whom I thought I could confide. I hoped to find some reassurance and a word of encouragement. Instead, my colleague suggested that all that had taken place at Dellrose was my fault and that I should look elsewhere for assurance and encouragement. That conversation pierced me to the core of my very being.

Now I could have taken that conversation in one of two ways: as a message from God declaring that no weapon against me shall prosper, or as an attempt by the devil to place fear in my heart. I chose to hear the message from God, believing as Paul wrote, "I am confident of this, that the one who began a good work among you will bring it to completion" (Philippians 1:6). I knew God would bring the work to completion, but for a split second I began to second-guess my calling as a pastor. Then it occurred to me that my colleague's church might be in the same predicament as Dellrose. And furthermore, it could be that my colleague was not familiar with the Dellrose neighborhood and how it had changed, allowing my colleague to move into a state of denial, accepting the maintenance mode as so many of our pastors do today—afraid of radical change.

If you find yourself doing something radical, such as transitioning and revitalizing a dying church, and people set out to crucify you, just remember, you are in great company. Daniel continued to pray; they put him in a lions den. The three Hebrew boys would not bow down; they put them in a fiery furnace. Job would not curse God; the devil took all that he had. And finally, Jesus knew he was the Son of God; they crucified him. All were vindicated, and God was glorified in the faithfulness of all.

God can take little and make much in the hands of those who believe that with God all things are possible. Even dry bones can live again. It is not about the size of your church; it is about believing in God. Remember, "faith is the assurance of things hoped for, the conviction of things not seen" (Hebrews 11:1). It is faith that has helped me thus far as the pastor of Dellrose United Methodist Church. I am a living witness that God will show up right on time. What makes things interesting is how God will remind you that God is still God while you find yourself going through the worst of the storm.

My prayer, for anyone reading this book who is doing something radical for God and finds him or herself in the midst of a lions den, a fiery furnace, catching hell from the devil, and being crucified on the cross, is this: Remember, God has not forsaken you. Help is on the way.

WHERE WE ARE TODAY

Today is July 2, 2006, the first Sunday of the month. It is a beautiful sunny day, and the parking lot is beginning to fill with people preparing for worship, which starts promptly at 10:30 A.M. every Sunday.

The greeters, who are part of the hospitality ministry, welcome the people as they walk up to the doors. The ushers, a team of eight or more, are in place to help guests and members find a place to sit. The orchestra, under the direction of the minister of music, plays praise music as the people gather for Sunday morning worship.

The choir members are in the choir room warming up. Children and adults are hurrying from Sunday school, knowing worship will begin soon. The worship team is going over the morning order of worship one last time in the conference room.

As the clock strikes 10:30 A.M., the worship leader, full of enthusiasm, stands in the pulpit and declares, "This is the day that the LORD has made; let us rejoice and be glad in it" (Psalm 118:24). Once the worship leader makes that statement, he or she invites the congregation to stand and give God praise. As the congregation stands, the choir processes into the worship center to the choir stand. Worship has begun!

Standing in the pulpit, I look out over a congregation of more than three hundred people, attending during the summer, just two days away from the July 4 holiday. It is a true testament of faith in God. Eight years ago, in the middle of the summer, when most people were on vacation, there might have been twenty-five people in attendance at a Sunday worship celebration here. Now there are more than three hundred; the choir has grown from four to thirty. A youth choir, which did not exist eight years ago, has twenty members today.

There were no musicians eight years ago; now there is a full orchestra: a drummer, pianist, percussionist, bass player, guitar player, electric pianist, and B-3 Hammond organ player. There was no office staff eight years ago. Now the church supports a full-time office administrator, part-time business administrator, part-time childcare director, part-time facility manager, part-time minister of music, part-time minister of orchestration, part-time choir director, part-time youth choir director, a host of volunteers, and four assistant-ministers-in-training, on track to be ordained pastors.

This is a special Sunday because it marks the beginning of my ninth year as pastor of Dellrose United Methodist Church. Not only does it mark the beginning of my ninth year, it is a reminder of how little can become much in the hands of God.

Just for the record, we are in the midst of the first phase of our four-phase building campaign. We are in the process of reconstructing our entire worship center—sanctuary and narthex. This first phase will cost a little over a quarter of a million dollars, and the money is in the bank. This demonstrates how God can take what was ineffective, unhealthy, and dying and turn it into effective, vital ministry.

With God's help, these bones live again! Amen.

NEW MEMBERS CLASS

New Members Orientation Agenda

12:00–12:10   REGISTRATION

12:10–12:20   OPENING PRAYER/ GREETINGS
                    ○ New Member Orientation Coordinator
                    ○ Pastor Harding and Staff
                    ○ What Attracted You to Dellrose?

12:20–12:50   WHAT IS THE CHURCH?
                    ○ The Body of Christ
                    ○ Five Biblical Purposes of the Church
                    ○ Salvation
                    ○ Sacraments
                    ○ Baptism
                    ○ The Lord's Supper

12:50–1:20   HOW WE DO MINISTRY
                    ○ Vision & Mission of Dellrose
                    ○ Why Do We Exist as a Church?
                    ○ Seven Bonds of Belonging
                    ○ Total Quality Ministry
                    ○ Dellrose Ministry Flow Chart

1:20–1:50   OUR STATEMENTS
                   ○ What We Believe
                   ○ The Apostles' Creed
                   ○ Dellrose Motto
                   ○ Dellrose Charge
                   ○ The Meaning of Membership & Membership Vows
                   ○ Benefits of Membership

1:50–2:20   BREAK

2:20–2:50   SUPPORTING OUR MISSION AND
                      MINISTRY
                   ○ What Is Stewardship?
                   ○ Tithing
                   ○ Commitment and Service Opportunities
                   ○ How Will You Support Ministry?
                   ○ Dellrose Ministry Structure
                   ○ United Methodist Church Structure

2:50–3:30   SPIRITUAL GIFTS ASSESSMENT

3:30–3:40   NEW MEMBER CLASS SURVEY

3:40–4:00   TOUR OF CHURCH/ CLOSING PRAYER/
                   DISMISSAL

JOB DESCRIPTIONS

Dellrose United Methodist Church Job Description

Ministry: Minister of Music

Principal Function

To prepare, promote, and enhance the spiritual atmosphere of all worship celebration through the ministry of music. To develop, supervise, and staff a music ministry that is relevant and helps Dellrose fulfill its vision, mission, and special events.

Responsibilities

1. Serve as a leader in the church's worship and praise.
2. Develop programs and ministries that enhance our appreciation for worship and music in the life of the church.
3. Attend staff meetings and report related activities regularly.
4. Serve as the first-level supervisor for all music staff.
5. Provide yearly performance evaluations for the music staff.
6. Responsible along with staff-parish for the hiring and, when necessary, the termination of all music staff according to the policies and procedures of Dellrose United Methodist Church.
7. Assist in creating an appropriate spiritual atmosphere conducive to powerful worship.
8. Assist praise team to lead the congregation in praise and congregational singing.
9. Plan and maintain a quality choir.

10. Ensure that all worship celebrations are appropriately staffed.
11. Schedule choirs for all worship celebrations, special days/events, and church engagements.
12. Report to Senior Pastor regularly on the areas of responsibility.

Accountability

- Senior Pastor
- Staff-Parish Relations Committee

Evaluation

Staff-Parish Relations Committee, in consultation with the Senior Pastor, shall evaluate.

Dellrose United Methodist Church
Job Description

Ministry: Adult Choir Director

Principal Function

To help the minister of music prepare, promote, and enhance the spiritual atmosphere of all worship celebrations through the ministry of music. To develop and supervise the choir so they may fulfill the Dellrose United Methodist Church vision and mission.

Responsibilities

1. Serve as a leader in the church's worship and praise.
2. Help develop and enhance the ministry of music for the life of the church.
3. Attend staff meetings and report related activities regularly.
4. Serve as a first-line supervisor in regard to the choir.
5. Assist in creating an appropriate spiritual atmosphere conducive to powerful worship.
6. Assist praise team in leading the congregation in praise and congregational singing.
7. Assist in ensuring that each choir is appropriately ready for all worship celebrations.
8. Report to Minister of Music regularly on the areas of responsibility.

Accountability

- Minister of Music
- Senior Pastor
- Staff-Parish Relations Committee

Evaluation

Staff-Parish Relations Committee, in consultation with Minister of Music and Senior Pastor, shall evaluate.

Dellrose United Methodist Church Job Description

Ministry: Minister of Orchestration and Musician Director

Principal Function

To help the Minister of Music by preparing, promoting, and enhancing the spiritual atmosphere of all worship celebration through the ministry of orchestration of all musicians. To develop and supervise the musicians so they may fulfill the Dellrose United Methodist Church vision and mission.

Responsibilities

1. Serve as a leader in the church's worship and praise.
2. Help develop and enhance the ministry of music for the life of the church.
3. Attend staff meetings and report related activities regularly.
4. Serve as a first-line supervisor in regard to the musicians.
5. Assist in creating an appropriate spiritual atmosphere conducive to powerful worship.
6. Assist praise team in leading the congregation in praise and congregational singing.
7. Ensure that each musician is appropriately ready for all worship celebrations.
8. Practice regularly with Minister of Music, choir directors, and musicians so all are of one accord.
9. Report to the Minister of Music regularly on the areas of responsibility.

Accountability

- Minister of Music
- Senior Pastor
- Staff-Parish Relations Committee

Evaluation

Staff-Parish Relations Committee, in consultation with Minister of Music and Senior Pastor, shall evaluate.

Dellrose United Methodist Church Job Description

Ministry: Youth Choir Director

Principal Function

To help the Minister of Music prepare, promote, and enhance the spiritual atmosphere of all youth worship celebrations through the ministry of music. To develop and supervise the youth choir so they may fulfill the Dellrose United Methodist Church vision and mission.

Responsibilities

1. Serve as a leader in the church's worship and praise.
2. Develop and enhance the ministry of the youth choir for the life of the church.
3. Attend staff meetings and report related activities regularly.
4. Help serve as a supervisor in regard to the youth choir.
5. Assist in creating an appropriate spiritual atmosphere conducive to powerful worship.
6. Assist praise team in leading the congregation in praise and congregational singing.
7. Ensure that youth choir is appropriately ready for youth Sunday worship celebration.
8. Report to Minister of Music regularly on the areas of responsibility.

Accountability

- Minister of Music
- Senior Pastor
- Staff-Parish Relations Committee

Evaluation

Staff-Parish Relations Committee, in consultation with Minister of Music and Senior Pastor, shall evaluate.

Dellrose United Methodist Church
Job Description

Ministry: Senior Pastor

Principal Function

The Senior Pastor shall oversee the total ministry of the local church in its nurturing ministries and in fulfilling its mission of witness and service outreach in the world by: (1) giving pastoral support, guidance, and training to the lay leadership in the local church, equipping them to fulfill the ministry to which they are sent as servants under the lordship of Christ; (2) providing ministry within the congregation and to the world; (3) ensuring faithful transmission of the Christian faith; (4) administering the temporal affairs of the congregation. In the context of these basic responsibilities, the Senior Pastor gives attention to four basic areas of duty:

Responsibilities

Preaching, Teaching, Worship
1. Preaching and teaching the Word of God.
2. Overseeing the worship life of the congregation.
3. Administering the sacraments.
4. Overseeing the total educational program of the church.
5. Leading the congregation in evangelistic outreach.
6. Instructing candidates for church membership.

Pastoral Care
1. Counseling those struggling with personal, ethical, or spiritual issues.
2. Visiting in the hospital and community.
3. Participating in the community and ecumenical concerns.
4. Searching out men and women for Christian vocations.
5. Giving leadership for discipleship in the world.

Equipping and Supervising
1. Ordering the life of the congregation.
2. Offering counsel and theological reflection.
3. Selecting, training, and deploying lay leadership.
4. Participating in denominational and ecumenical programs.
5. Assuming supervisory responsibilities within the connection.

Administration
1. Being the administrative officer.
2. Being responsible for goal setting and planning.
3. Administering the provisions of the *Discipline*.
4. Giving an account of pastoral ministries.

Accountability

- District Superintendent
- Staff-Parish Relations Committee

Evaluation

Staff-Parish Relations Committee shall complete evaluation within the guidelines as set forth by the Kansas West Conference.

Dellrose United Methodist Church
Job Description

Ministry: Office Administrator

Principal Function

To manage the day-to-day operations of the church office as well as see to the completion of all other clerical responsibilities for the church. To aid the Senior Pastor in his/her ministry in the areas of Church Administration, Record Keeping, Membership Records, and the Scheduling of Appointments.

Responsibilities

1. Ensure the up-to-date maintaining and ordering of the files and membership records of the church.
2. Ensure the preparation of the weekly worship folders for Dellrose Worship Celebration as well as other newsletters and programs for ministry and worship at Dellrose.
3. Sort and distribute church mail in an orderly and timely manner.
4. Coordinate and serve as support personnel for programming ministries of the church.
5. Attend weekly Church Staff meeting and Church Council.
6. See to the coordination and execution of church-wide mailings.
7. Keep office running with training and management of office volunteers.
8. Place orders and keep records of supplies of the church office.
9. To help keep track of speaking engagements and other appointments on the calendar of the Senior Pastor.
10. To help with writing correspondence, and any other clerical duties for the Senior Pastor.
11. To work with the membership secretaries in keeping the membership records of the church by entering the data and keeping all information current.
12. To supervise the completion of the conference year-end statistical reports.
13. To distribute and keep records of funds for those needing missions help from the church.

14. Help facilitate the Senior Pastor's responsibilities with the annual conference, district, and general church and community involvement.
15. Other duties as assigned by Senior Pastor.

Accountability

- Senior Pastor
- Staff-Parish Relations Committee

Evaluation

Staff-Parish Relations Committee, in consultation with the Senior Pastor, shall complete evaluation within the guidelines as set forth in the Dellrose employee handbook.

Dellrose United Methodist Church Job Description

Ministry: Business Administrator

Principal Function

To assist the Senior Pastor in the area of Finance Administration so that he/she may be free to attend to the spiritual leadership of the congregation.

Responsibilities

1. Manage the finance and business affairs of the church.
2. Serve as a member of the staff.
3. Assist appropriate persons in executing the finance management of the church (e.g., Finance Committee Chairperson, Board of Trustees, etc.).
4. Assist Finance Committee and Senior Pastor in preparing budget for the church.
5. Monitor expenses during the year to keep within the framework of the church's budget.
6. Supervise the bookkeeping of the operating budget and funds coming into and through the church.
7. Ensure all bills, church obligations, and mission and ministry funds are paid on time, provided funds are available.
8. Assist Financial Secretaries and Finance Assistant to ensure that members contributions are recorded and financial statements are issued on time.
9. Prepare church payroll.
10. Prepare staff salary information and maintain knowledge in the areas of pension funds, health and life insurance, FICA, federal and state income taxes, etc.
11. Monitor expenditures according to budgetary authorization.
12. Direct the writing of checks for budgeted items and specific line items up to the amount budgeted.
13. Direct bidding process, purchases and maintenance of all supplies, equipment and services for the church, working in conjunction with the Board of Trustees, Committee on Finance, and church staff.
14. Serve as a liaison to the Committee on Finance.
15. Serve as an ex officio member of the Board of Trustees.

16. Work with Church Council on all legal matters regarding the church.
17. Attend staff meetings and Church Council, providing written reports.
18. Meet with Senior Pastor on financial status of the church.
19. Assist in other administrative functions as directed by the Senior Pastor and/or the Staff-Parish Relations Committee.

Accountability

- Senior Pastor
- Staff-Parish Relations Committee

Membership

- Church Council and Executive Committee
- Committee on Finance
- Board of Trustees (ex officio member)

Evaluation

Staff-Parish Relations Committee, in consultation with the Senior Pastor, shall complete evaluation within the guidelines as set forth in the Dellrose employee handbook.

Dellrose United Methodist Church
Job Description

Ministry: Childcare Director

Principal Function

The Childcare Director will provide leadership for the Childcare Ministry to create an environment that nurtures spiritual, mental, and physical growth of infants and children under the care of Dellrose's ministry. The director will ensure that Dellrose nursery and childcare policies are fulfilled in order to provide a safe, risk-free environment for infants and children.

Responsibilities

1. Ensure the planning and implementation of a weekly program.
2. Ensure the planning and implementation for spiritual and educational development.
3. Prepare and maintain needed materials and supplies.
4. Provide supervision and evaluation for the Nursery and Childcare Ministry.
5. Manage the nursery and childcare personnel and attend to administrative details.
6. Enforce nursery and childcare rules and regulations.
7. Maintain a professional attitude.
8. Treat all persons with dignity and respect.
9. Attend to disciplinary actions according to policies and procedures.
10. Attend continuing education events.
11. Attend weekly staff meetings.
12. Meet weekly with Senior Pastor.
13. Attend church-related meetings and leadership events.
14. Hold regular nursery and childcare staff meetings.
15. Assist in the planning and attend meetings with childcare team monthly or as needed.
16. Other duties as assigned by the Senior Pastor.

Accountability

- Senior Pastor
- Staff-Parish Relations Committee

Evaluation

Staff-Parish Relations Committee, in consultation with the Senior Pastor, shall complete evaluation within the guidelines as set forth in the Dellrose employee handbook.

Dellrose United Methodist Church
Job Description

Ministry: Facilities Manager

Principal Function

The Facilities Manager is to oversee the day-to-day maintenance and upkeep of the Dellrose grounds and facility. The Facilities Manager will have the church and education building ready for worship celebration, all classes, programs and special events.

Responsibilities

1. To ensure the opening, closing, and securing of the church and education building at all functions and activities.
2. Report any malfunctions as necessary to Senior Pastor and Chairperson of Trustees Board.
3. Maintain an inside and outside inspection of the church and education building in order to detect any damages or items that need to be reported and repaired.
4. Order all supplies that are necessary for maintenance of the building in a timely manner.
5. Help set up tables and chairs for scheduled functions with appropriate notification.
6. Help maintain the cleaning of the entire church building on the inside and outside.
7. Attend weekly church staff meetings and Church Council.
8. Meet with the Senior Pastor weekly.
9. Setting controls for temperature.
10. Change lightbulbs when needed.
11. Clean all restrooms, offices, and classrooms. Clean kitchen, fellowship hall, and sanctuary when needed, but inspect daily. Empty all trash receptacles on a daily basis.
12. To perform other duties as assigned by the Senior Pastor.

Accountability

- Senior Pastor
- Staff-Parish Relations Committee

Evaluation

Staff-Parish Relations Committee, in consultation with the Senior Pastor, shall complete evaluation within the guidelines as set forth in the Dellrose employee handbook.

NOTES

Introduction—When Little Is Much

1. *The Book of Discipline of The United Methodist Church 1996* (Nashville: The United Methodist Publishing House, 1996), Para. 212.1, Section IV: "Churches in transitional communities," 120.

1. The Main Thing

1. Leander E. Keck, ed., *The New Interpreter's Bible Commentary: Volume VI* (Nashville: Abingdon Press, 2001), 1499.
2. Ibid.
3. Leander E. Keck, ed., *The New Interpreter's Bible Commentary: Volume I* (Nashville: Abingdon Press, 2001), 827.
4. Ibid.
5. Ibid., 827–28.
6. Ibid., 828.

2. Pastor and Parish—Two Stories Converge

1. Jim Collins, *Good to Great: Why Some Companies Make the Leap . . . and Others Don't* (New York: HarperCollins Publishers, 2001), 1.
2. Ibid.
3. From the "Dellrose United Methodist Historical Record Book" (unpublished), 1.
4. *The Book of Discipline*, 120.

3. Reaching the Lost—Rebuilding Worship

1. Carlyle Fielding Stewart III, *African American Church Growth* (Nashville: Abingdon Press, 1994), 41.

2. Louis F. Benson, *The Hymnody of the Christian Church* (John Knox Press, 1956, reprinted from New York: George H. Doran Co., 1927), 240–41.

3. Nancy T. Ammerman and Carl S. Dudley, *Congregations in Transition* (San Francisco: Jossey-Bass, 2002), 10.

4. Teaching the Found—Rebuilding Discipleship

1. Eugene H. Peterson, *Working the Angles: The Shape of Pastoral Integrity* (Grand Rapids: Eerdmans, 1987), 1.

2. Ibid., 2.

3. Ibid.

4. Debi Childers's story is used by permission.

5. Les Smith's quotation is used by permission.

6. Carol Wertz's quotation and story are used by permission.

7. Stephen A. Macchia, *Becoming a Healthy Church: 10 Characteristics* (Grand Rapids: Baker Books, 1999), 80–81; the list of eight key concepts is summarized from Robert E. Coleman's *The Master Plan of Evangelism* (Grand Rapids: Revell, 1979).

5. Sending the Taught—Rebuilding Ministry

1. Carol Wertz's quotation is used by permission.

2. Otto F. Crumroy Jr., Stan Kukawka, and Frank N. Witman, *Church Administration and Finance Manual: Resources for Leading the Local Church* (Harrisburg: Morehouse Publishing, 1998), 133.